TREASURE WITHIN

Rediscovering the Mystics

GW00360372

for

Damien

Michael J Cunningham SDB

©Don Bosco Publications 2011
Thornleigh House
Sharples Park
BOLTON BL1 6PQ
Email: **joyce@salesians.org.uk**
www.don-bosco-publications.co.uk
ISBN 9780954838831

Contents

Introduction

In the secret of my heart teach me wisdom. (Ps 51)

There is a subtle but profound shift taking place in our times. We live in a very busy, highly extraverted, culture that fills us with all kinds of information and endless entertainment, yet there is a hunger in our souls that our technical brilliance cannot fill. It has always been the task of great religions to feed this hunger, but some of our institutional Churches struggle to meet this need. Our Churches are strong in terms of what Ken Wilber calls the tasks of the first half of life. We find doctrines, rituals and moral guidance to help us to build up our egos, and we get a sense of belonging and of identity. The problem is that we can do all this and still see God as distant from us, looking on from afar, checking our faults and failings, and never quite satisfied with our performance, however hard we try. Our busyness and willpower never seem to be enough. Not only that, but this distant God, who we are told is a God of love, seems determined to punish us.

The task of healthy religion is to shatter this toxic image of God and shatter our egotistic sense of self and totally transform our lives. We are invited to move from the dualistic sense that God is distant and apart, to a life of union and intimacy. While the need for moral guidelines and external authority always remains, it should be as a support to the inner authority of a personal and intimate experience of God as a loving Father, to use Jesus' preferred way of speaking about God. This is the way of the saints and the mystics who invite us to move beyond simple certainties into the profound mystery of infinite love that surrounds us every moment of every day.

In this book I am hoping to invite you to undertake this journey. It is not easy. Sometimes we prefer to say our prayers, even attend church services, perhaps even study some theology, but we want to keep the ego in control of all this. We want to feel good about ourselves. The mystics invite us to go beyond the question of worthiness, performance religion, or religion as a set of requirements to surrender to a religion of relationship. It requires a recognition that life is not perfect, and a holding of the tension between the light and the dark in everything, including ourselves. The price is the death of our egotistic ways so that we can enter the new life of Christ.

In part one (chapters 1-10) I have tried to invite you into the mystery of your life in God. This is our true identity. Once we realise it, everything changes. We look out at the world with different eyes. We discover how deeply we are united to God, not by our own efforts but by the gift of transforming grace. We begin to taste what St Paul meant when he said *I live no longer, Christ lives in me.* We learn to move from the separate self that always wants to judge others in a dualistic way. We learn to live in a non-dual way that doesn't deny differences but looks at the foundational fact of *being,* that we all share in God. This leads us into the spirituality of compassion, forgiveness and inclusion. Even the traditional distinction in the Church between the active and contemplative life is seen as less important than the task of integrating the two, so that we can become active contemplatives.

I have tried to explore key aspects of this journey of transformation: the call of mystery, the need to go from control to surrender to this loving mystery, the need to re-enchant our world by uniting sacred and secular, the question of our true identity as sons and daughters of God, the shift from the spirituality of perfection of recent years to the spirituality of imperfection, the need to accept the ambiguity and contradictions not just of the world we live in, but in our own souls. As we learn to forgive ourselves, we learn to forgive others. As we open ourselves to God's forgiving love, we begin to experience that love flowing through us.

We cannot achieve transformation; it is the work of the Holy Spirit in our souls. God never forces himself on us, but he invites us to open the door, to enter through the narrow gate to discover the treasure within which is the divine indwelling. What we are asked to do is to slip out of our external world of activity and busyness from time to time, on a daily basis ideally, and to enter our inner world in silent prayer, where, as Jesus promises, the Father is already waiting for us.

In part two of the book (chapters 11-15) I have chosen to write about five people who have touched my life and given me the confidence to embark on this journey. They have deeply explored the contemplative journey. They have written about it, and they invite us to follow them. I begin with Thomas Merton who has been a key figure in the recovery of the mystical contemplative tradition in the Western Church. He was prepared to open himself to the Eastern religions such as Buddhism and Hinduism, at a time when this was rare in Catholic circles. He also reconnected silent prayer with action and concern for the social evils of his time. Julian of Norwich was Merton's favourite English mystic and she was probably the first woman to write a book in English. She has a beautifully compassionate spirituality, revealing that God is incapable of anger; when we fail, He looks at us with pity not with blame. She freely speaks of the fatherhood and the motherhood of God.

Thérèse of Lisieux is a universally popular saint whose gift to the Church was the discovery of her *Little Way* which is rooted in the spirituality of imperfection. She wrote her spiritual autobiography on the orders of her superior and it became perhaps the biggest-selling spiritual book of the twentieth century. For Thérèse, it all comes down to love, as is true of all the mystics. Our failings do not keep God from us; they are the place where we meet the mercy of God. Bede Griffiths was an English Benedictine who went to live in India to find the other half of his soul. Like Merton he sought a marriage between East and West and he explored the developing spiritual consciousness that unites the masculine with the feminine. John O'Donohue, an Irish philosopher-poet sought to move the Church out of an excessive reliance on moral strictures, hierarchy, rules and regulation towards a recovery of the more mystical tradition which he explored in the context of Celtic spirituality. He saw the recovery of the sense of Beauty in the union of sacred and secular.

These men and women invite us to undertake the great adventure of the human soul. While the twentieth century marked the exploration of outer space, the twenty-first century is leading us into a new consciousness, a journey within that moves beyond the dualism of the Western mind to the unifying vision that is at the heart of all true religion. It is what Jesus called the one thing necessary: the kingdom of God. The lives of these five people point to the vision and experience of all the mystics: oneness with God, oneness with others, oneness with creation. I hope this little book encourages you to embark on this journey to explore what Jesus meant when he said:

Seek and you will find.

Chapter 1 — The Call of Mystery

The Christian of the future will be a mystic or he or she will not exist at all, if by mysticism we mean a genuine experience of God emerging at the very heart of our existence.[1]

All we can be certain about, these days, is the fact of change. This paradox lies at the heart of our culture. We are in times of transition and its effects are everywhere. We face immense challenges. Although we live in a global village, we are unable to rid the world of war and violence. Our political leaders struggle to grasp the challenge of global warming. The Western economic system, which seemed to be delivering more and more prosperity to the favoured nations, has crashed; with severe consequences for the whole world. We all live under the threat of international terrorism. The communications revolution swamps us with information overload, yet we seem to lack wisdom.

Times of transition are very challenging. In the past, religion and the Church provided a safe haven of stability, in the face of change. Today, however, the Church, like all institutions, is caught up in the middle of rapid change. Western Christian Churches have been hit by falling numbers. The Catholic Church has seen a large and significant fall in priestly and religious vocations. Churches are being closed or amalgamated. Congregations appear increasingly elderly, although in some countries immigration has recently boosted church attendances.

The Catholic Church has also been devastated by the sexual abuse crisis. Though it can be pointed out that child abuse is a problem for society as well as the Church, and, statistically, the percentage of priests involved is small. Nevertheless it is significant and widespread, and it has caused deep pain and anguish to so many. It has been an appalling betrayal of trust by a religious body that has frequently tried

---

1 Karl Rahner *The Practice of Faith: A Handbook of Contemporary Spirituality* (London SCM Press, 1985) p22

to take the moral high ground in matters of sexuality. The attempt by various members of the hierarchy to cover up these abuses has only compounded the pain and sense of betrayal.

Alongside the pain there is deep anger felt by many inside and outside the Church. On a recent visit to Ireland, I was told of Sisters who were spat at in the street after the publication of the Ryan Report into systematic levels of violence and cruelty inflicted in many institutions run by Catholic religious orders. For many good priests, religious, and faithful laity this is a wound that all of us carry at this time.

The Church is clearly in need of reform, but not just at the level of structures and organisation; though I think there is a real need for a less hierarchical and a more community-shaped structure that encourages dialogue and sharing of responsibilities; and the contribution of women has to be re-examined. I want to suggest that the crisis in the Church is not unconnected with the crisis in our world and in our culture. The Church can have a significant part to play, but only if it connects with what is happening at a deeper level in the wider world.

There are signs that a real revolution is taking place in our world. It is not a political revolution, bringing in new structures; although these may flow from it. It is a revolution in *consciousness*. It is a spiritual revolution which is slowly emerging in the lives of people who are truly open and aware. At its heart it will provide us with a new way of seeing and a new way of being, that can move us out of the current dualistic ways of seeing, to an appreciation of a more unified picture. This is really what authentic religion should be about, but sadly many of the religions, not just Christianity, seem to have forgotten their true purpose. In fact religion seems adept at creating divisions. There are over 30,000 different Christian denominations. Without a shift to a higher level of consciousness, we will not be able to free ourselves from the trap of oppositional thinking that divides rather than unites.

Oppositional thinking is rooted in the binary mind which is our normal way of thinking, *This is not that, that is not this.* The binary mind is rooted in the opposites that we find around us: light and dark, good and bad, right and wrong and so on. It is essentially dualistic. I recently returned from the United States where I found political opinion heavily polarised between liberal and conservative media-driven agenda. A lot of heat was being generated; but nobody seemed to be listening. The United Nations have recently uncovered evidence of mass killings of Hutus by Tutsis in the Congo in revenge for the mass killings of Tutsis by Hutus in Rwanda. Israelis and Palestinians have still not been able to resolve their differences without violence. The war in Afghanistan rumbles on, as does the violence in Iraq.

At its best, religion should offer a way to resolve these conflicts by peaceful means and reconciliation; in some cases this has been successful. In reality, if we are honest, we find that religion often adds fuel to the fire in many of these disputes, and this has been true throughout history. Religious believers seem no different from others; they are equally trapped in the dualistic mind of who is right and who is wrong, who has the correct formulas and who hasn't. If you add the conviction that God is on *our* side then it leads to even more blind justification for excluding and condemning others, and even justifying violence in God's name.

If we are to really reform and renew religion, we have to move beyond this damaging dualistic mindset to a non-dual way of seeing and living. The monotheistic religions, Christianity, Judaism and Islam, all seem trapped at the same level. We Christians seem to have forgotten that Jesus was essentially a non-dual teacher. He wanted us to move from simplistic *either/or* judgments to a more inclusive *both/and* mindset. That is why he begins his ministry by telling us that we need to undergo a radical change, a *metanoia*, which implies a new way of looking, seeing and thinking if we are to understand the good news he has come to proclaim. Without that we will continue to put the new wine into the old wineskins, as many religious believers still do.

Jesus is trying to move us to a deeper level of spiritual consciousness. He presents the spiritual journey not as a set of certainties, but as an invitation to embrace *mystery*. This mystery is full of mercy, com-passion, forgiveness and inclusion. Jesus speaks of God as his loving

Father and invites us to have faith in Him. The mystery that Jesus reveals is forgiving and inclusive, not judgmental and exclusive as many religious believers seem to prefer.

We have to admit that we have seriously distorted the message. If you ask the average Catholic what faith is; they will, more than likely, refer to a set of beliefs and doctrines. I remember, growing up as a young Catholic, being taught in school to learn all the answers in the penny catechism. Everyone was taught in the same way. There wasn't much talk about a spiritual journey; we were on a way of certainty. We Catholics had the truth. In a sense, the journey was over before it began. If we Catholics had the truth it meant that everybody else was wrong. It certainly reinforced the dualistic mind. No room for mystery at all, *Job done*, as we say these days. The Catholic faith I grew up in was about certainty not mystery. In fact we rejoiced in our certainty, *We had the truth*. The others clearly didn't.

Today we are recovering a better understanding of faith and spirituality. Karl Rahner pointed the way when he suggested that the Church of the future would have to rediscover its mystical tradition. There are encouraging signs that this is happening as we move beyond faith as certainty to an embrace of mystery. This will not be easy; it will demand spiritual maturity. In St Paul's language, it means moving from a diet of baby milk to solid food, as Jeremy Young explains:

> Certainty is hugely appealing to the devout because it promises to take away their anxiety through guaranteeing the truth of what they believe, and, hence their acceptance by God. It provides the emotional reassurance they require. However, any assertion of certainty whether by individuals or institutions is a huge problem for the contemporary Church because it is a betrayal of genuine Christian faith.[2]

What Jeremy Young underlines is that faith is more about trust than certainty. This is the way Jesus speaks about faith in the gospels.

---

2 Jeremy Young *The Cost of Certainty* (Darton, Longman and Todd London 2004) p5

He asks people to trust in the unconditional love of his Father. At no point does Jesus set out a list of doctrinal statements. The same is true in the Old Testament, with figures such as Abraham and Moses who were asked to put their complete trust in Yahweh. Sadly the Church has turned biblical faith on its head and reduced the great faith-adventure—the great spiritual journey, into a security blanket of certainty. The purpose of the religion in which I was educated was more about getting us as individuals into the next world. We even had an easy mechanism called the *Nine First Fridays.*[3]

You can see how the mystical tradition got squeezed out of such a picture. It never died out, but the Protestant Reformation and the rationalism of the enlightenment left it badly wounded and sidelined. We fought each other and even killed each other about who had the right theological formulas. Trapped in our dualistic minds, we forgot the central point of the teaching of Jesus about love, compassion, forgiveness and inclusion. I am writing these words on a most historic day when Pope Benedict XVI has visited Lambeth Palace in London and been warmly greeted by the Archbishop of Canterbury. Later they took part in an ecumenical service in Westminster Abbey, in the presence of Anglican and Catholic bishops sitting together.

I was struck by Pope Benedict's reminder that what unites us is far greater than what divides us and by Archbishop Williams' quote from Edward Pusey that *it is our lack of holiness which is keeping us apart.* Chief Rabbi Sacks has suggested that Europe has become more secularised, not because it lost faith in God but because it lost faith in the ability of believers to live peacefully together. I think that these remarks by the leaders of the Catholic, Anglican, and Jewish community point the way to a new spirituality that can move beyond dualism and antagonism. This doesn't minimise the very real differences, but is does underline the relational quality of all authentic spirituality. It is a relationship that moves us towards the underlying unity for which Jesus prayed.

---

3 The promise of not dying without receiving the Sacraments, if you went to Mass and received Holy Communion on nine consecutive First Fridays.

Today, unity is being recovered in a silent but very powerful spiritual revolution in our world; but there are dangers. There is a very real split today between religion and spirituality. If this split is to be healed for the benefit of both, the institutional Church needs to open itself to its own mystical tradition. Mysticism allows us to deal with differences; not by ignoring them, but by grasping the greater truth that can emerge in the reconciling of opposites with love. Mysticism is not just a way of praying. It grows from the realisation that prayer is the necessary software that moves us out of the everyday egotistic mindset that always wants to divide, to compare and to control.

Thomas Merton is rightly credited as being one of the most influential people in reviving the contemplative way of life in the Western Church. Towards the end of his life, he got permission from his Cistercian Order to travel to Asia which had held on to the mystical tradition. Sadly he was to die there in a tragic accident, but not before he had written to his community of monks to say that whatever he was discovering in the East we already possessed in our Western tradition; but it had been largely forgotten and buried in the past. Even the contemplative orders had forgotten the contemplative tradition. They had reduced prayer to saying prayers.

Contemplative prayer is not just a way of praying. It is a way of seeing. It is a new way of being. It opens us up to the holy mystery that surrounds us, every moment of our lives. It should be the task of religion to lead us into this mystery. All religions need some kind of structure, some pattern of authority in which to frame the religious search. The opportunities for private delusion are many, especially if we think we have a private hotline to God. But the point of the structure is to enable the journey into the mystery of God to take place. It is there to facilitate not to stifle. Part of the decline in institutional religions today is due to an unbalanced reliance on the masculine structure of order, discipline, reason, rules and a hierarchy which prefers a quiet unquestioning obedience from the faithful. This is especially true in the Catholic Church. This approach is no longer feeding the hunger that many people feel in their souls, especially in a world that is largely dominated by technology. Technology is good and very useful at times, but it doesn't nourish the deepest part of our humanity. It has nothing to say about our desires for love, wonder, acceptance, meaning and purpose. It doesn't speak to our loneliness and longings. It doesn't address our joys and our sorrows.

Healthy religion needs to recover a way of inviting people into the mystery of God. In many ways we have said too much about God. We have sought to define and control God. This, of course, reduces the transcendence and the splendour of the holy mystery to the level of our own minds and rational intelligence. We have domesticated God, to fit our own agenda. I remember listening to a talk by a Catholic bishop entitled, *Our God is too small.* Unfortunately the words he used seemed to make God even smaller. His was very much a Catholic God; and simply reinforced an easy dismissal of those we lumped together as *Non-Catholics.*

I think that we are being asked today to go beyond this dualistic mindset that all too easily presumes that we have the truth and therefore others do not. We are being invited to move from a controlling spirituality to a spirituality of surrender. Surrendering to mystery is not something that we can achieve for ourselves. That is why it is such a profound challenge to the Western mind for both religious believers and non-believers. The secular mindset, with all its achievements, doesn't satisfy our hunger for union. Sadly, too much contemporary religion seems to keep us trapped in the divisions and comparisons of the dualistic mind:

Who is worthy and who is unworthy?
Who is in and who is out?
Who is good and who is bad?
Who do I approve of and who do I disapprove of?

The recovery of the contemplative tradition reminds us that the spiritual journey may be difficult and challenging to the way we normally think and feel, but it reveals the incredibly consoling truth that the gift of union is already given. We don't have to strive for it; for that would be another sign of the ego asserting control of the journey. All we have to do is to surrender to the mystery of infinite unconditional love that surrounds us at every moment. It is a case of becoming truly aware of and truly present to a gracious mystery. It is a journey into love.

Chapter 2 — Following the Mystics

The problem for most of us is that we don't realize how united we are with God.[4]

One of the signs of hunger for God, experienced in our times, is the renewed interest in the lives and teachings of the mystics. In the second part of this book I want to present brief portraits of some of these men and women who have influenced my own spiritual journey. The mystics are not always easy to read. They are trying to find words to describe what cannot be described—a direct experience of God. They stretch language in ways that sometimes worries theologians. They are the poets of the spiritual life. Some of them may appear to be a bit extreme in their life-styles. What can they have to say that would be of interest to us who live in a very different world?

Another difficulty is that mysticism has not always been seen as part of the mainstream of Christian theology and teaching. As we saw in the first chapter, Christianity has too often failed to lead spiritual searchers beyond dualistic consciousness. Even in teaching about prayer, there has been little or no reference to the mystical tradition. As I underwent my own training, as a Salesian, I cannot recall any teaching about the mystical tradition. I was instructed to meditate but never to contemplate. In preaching retreats to a whole range of religious in different parts of the world in recent years I have heard the same story. There is growing evidence of spiritual hunger today. The Holy Spirit is awakening many souls to become aware of the great gift we have all been given as human beings: that God dwells in the very core of our souls and we have all been created to live in conscious union with him. So we need to ask the question, *What is it that the mystics teach us about the spiritual journey?*

Mystics are people whose lives have been transformed into a realised oneness with God, a realised oneness with others and a realised

---

4 Gerald May, *The Dark Night of the Soul* (Harper San Francisco 2005) p44

oneness with creation. In this sense they have gone beyond the sense of separation which is the fruit of dualism. Mystics have gone beyond the autonomous self which sees itself in a defensive position before reality. Dualism creates opposition and emphasises differences. Mysticism proclaims the fundamental unity of all, the connectedness that lies at the heart of everything. Mystics welcome reality as it is. They are truly present to what is. Dualism confronts reality by wanting to shape it to fit the point of view of the ego. The separate self is necessarily built on anxiety and fear. When Jesus uses the word *faith* in the gospels he is asking us to trust the mystery. For Jesus, the opposite of faith is not unbelief; it is anxiety and fear.

The question of identity is at the heart of the spiritual journey. Too often religion places the spiritual journey in a moralising framework. From that perspective the key question is whether I can make myself worthy in the eyes of God. Religion seems to supply the answer by offering doctrines to believe in, a pattern of moral behaviour, and a set of rituals to practice. If I can succeed in these areas, I can win God's favour and get admitted to heaven after death.

This is *religion as requirements* or *performance religion* and it shapes the lives of most Christians. Unfortunately it is an illusion and it seriously distorts the image of God that Jesus came to reveal. It leaves us separate from God who is reduced to a great examiner in the sky, who is watching our every move and recording our every sin. And, of course, we all find, as St Paul reminds us in Romans chapter seven, that none of us can reach the state of moral perfection. Imperfection and failure are written into the human condition. Even the great saints demonstrated human weaknesses; they also lived part of their lives in the false self. The four gospels portray the frequent failures and disagreements among Jesus' closest followers, including such towering foundational figures as Peter and Paul.

The mystics offer a different perspective. For them the spiritual journey is not a question of moral striving, of wilful effort, of personal achievement. The mystics would say that we don't have to struggle to win God's favour because we already have it. The gift of union with

God is already given. The spiritual journey is much more about willingness rather than wilfulness; it is a surrendering to the holy mystery of God's unconditional love. It is much more about falling in love than striving to be good. Our moral behaviour is, of course, important, but it follows on from our surrender to God's compassionate and forgiving love. Rather than concentrating on attempts to please God, the mystics bask in his unconditional love. *Religion as requirements* is replaced by *religion as relationship*. The God of the mystics seeks intimacy rather than moral perfection, as Ian Petit points out in a beautiful little book, *God is not Angry*:

> The fact that we get wrong ideas about God should not alarm us. The apostles had difficulty in trying to understand Jesus. They lived with him and listened to his teaching, but their ideas of him were only formed slowly.[5]

We shouldn't expect ourselves to be different. Jesus is speaking to us from a very high level of spiritual consciousness.

The spiritual journey is our awakening to the holy mystery of love that surrounds us. It is much less about finding God than being found by God. It is much more about presence to that mystery than moral striving. It is a surrender of control. The mystics speak about receptivity. We never initiate the journey; it is always a response to what we have received.

Some months ago I was in South Africa preaching a series of retreats to the Sisters of Nazareth. The Sisters work mostly with the sick and elderly, but in Cape Town they have a special unit caring for abandoned babies. During the course of the year they had taken in 103 children and managed to return 97 of them to their extended family members, foster care or adoption. While I was there, Sr Margaret, who is in charge of the unit, asked me if I would baptise a baby, who was not expected to live very long. He was the child of an alcoholic mother. He was given the name *Damien* since he arrived in the care of the Sisters on the day Fr Damien, the priest who worked with lepers of Molokai,

---

5 Ian Petit, *God is not angry* (Darton Longman & Todd 1997) p22

was beatified. I baptised Damien on Thursday evening and he died on the following Sunday. During the ceremony of baptism the priest anoints the breast of the child. I have always been struck by the profound significance of this action. It is really an anointing of the heart and it signifies that the person being baptised has been created by God to receive love and to give love. This is the whole purpose of our existence.

As I blessed the heart of this vulnerable child struggling and fighting a losing battle for life I was deeply moved by the vulnerability of love. In a few days of life what had this child achieved? I can personally testify that little Damien communicated love to me in a way that is not easy to put into words, I often think of that child, especially when I am facing difficulties. I pray to him and I see him as an angel that watches over me, and I have written this book in his memory. For me he was an image of both the power and the vulnerability of love. To expose our vulnerability to another is very challenging. We can be deeply hurt by rejection. This child rejected by his mother, in a very real way symbolised the way Jesus was rejected by the people and both civil and religious authorities. His love was not diminished by rejection. His love overcame it by an extraordinary act of forgiveness on the cross. Here again we encounter the mystery of paradox in a God who prefers weakness over strength.

The mystics teach us not to be afraid of vulnerability and human frailty. Sometimes, when we look at their lives, it appears that they are on a different plane. In part two of this book (chapters 11-15) I want to show how they all faced difficulties of one sort or another. St Thérèse of Lisieux, for example, went through a long period of darkness, with no felt experience of God's love. It lasted right up until her death. The spiritual journey is not an easy one. That is why so many of us find that we are unable to give up control and surrender to a mystery of love that we can never understand. We are not in control.

The National Gallery in London contains a painting of *The Adoration of the Kings* by Pieter Bruegel the Elder. As the gift of the myrrh—the ointment of death—is offered by one of the magi the Christ Child recoils in fear. The painting is a disturbing reminder of the vulnerability of love. Good art invites us to look in a contemplative fashion. I have no artistic training, but I love to look at art. It speaks to the deepest level of heart and soul. True seeing can be worth more than thousands of words.

St Thomas Aquinas and St John of the Cross, both brilliant theologians, remind us that we cannot really know God with our minds, but only through love. This is not an easy message for people of our times, who are all children of the enlightenment. Our rational minds can only take us so far on the road to mystery. It is not necessary to be highly educated to make the spiritual journey. In fact too much Western education simply reinforces the dualistic mind. Our minds can only take us so far. If we move to contemplative prayer we have to learn a different kind of mind, a different way of seeing. Jesus suggests, that to embrace the new consciousness of the kingdom, we have to leave the sophistication of our minds behind and become like little children:

> Truly I tell you, whoever does not receive the kingdom of God as a little child will never enter it.[6]

When Peter answers Jesus' question about his identity correctly, Jesus tells him that flesh and blood has not revealed this to him but his Father in heaven. Jesus is pointing to a different kind of knowledge that spiritual teachers call *wisdom*. Clearly our minds can take us towards the mystery but they tend to keep us at the level of egotistic consciousness that keeps us separate and distinct. We look at everything from our own point of view and try to shape everyone else to fit that limited perspective. What wisdom does is to reveal a different kind of knowing, a knowing of the heart.

Despite all the contemporary emphasis on rugged individualism, we cannot carry the mystery on our own. We want to work it out in our head, we want answers. We judge everything from our own personal perspective. How will this affect me? What will I get out of this? The *private* is not spacious enough. If we are honest, most of us get a kind

---

6 Mark 10:15

18

of sense of this so we join groups of like-minded people, to satisfy our human need for belonging. Sadly a lot of faith communities stay at this level, where it is all about our group, our religion our nation, our ways of doing things, all of which enforce the way we see and perceive those who are different.

In my own contact with asylum seekers, I see rejection written into their faces. The argument is always that of scarcity. *There isn't enough of our wealth to include these people. Why don't they go back to where they came from?* Even church-going Christians often think this way which underlines how little transformation has taken place on their spiritual journey. I was speaking recently to a Salesian priest in the USA in a parish with a significant Hispanic population, so the parish provides Mass in English and in Spanish. On the feast of Pentecost, when the readings celebrate the great unity of believers that transcends language and culture, he celebrated a bilingual Mass in English and in Spanish. The result was some of the English-speaking parishioners walked out.

If we are honest we all struggle to accept the other, the one who is different from me. We are all influenced to some degree by the scarcity model. Jesus tried everything he could to move his followers beyond this. He reached out to tax collectors and sinners, to Romans, to the Canaanite woman. He reached out beyond his own family, he refused to cast fire on a Samaritan village that was inhospitable, and he always reached out beyond his own people. In all of this he is trying to reveal to us what his Father is like, who causes *his sun to rise on good people as well as bad and his rain to fall on just and unjust alike.*

What Jesus is asking from us and what the mystics experience is a transformation of consciousness that reveals everything is one. For Jesus it is never about scarcity; it is always about abundance. With Jesus there are always twelve baskets of extra food, or six water jars with twenty gallons of wine! God is about abundance and the mystics are the ones who get it, because they live at the level of deepest being, which is a gift not an attainment. Everyone and everything in creation participates in the gift of being. Everything and everyone is sustained by the holy mystery which always lies beyond us, but is at the same time accessible in everyday reality. This transcendent mystery of God appears to us in Jesus, in human form. The Incarnation is God's holiness appearing in flesh and blood. The mystery becomes visible, the ordinary becomes extraordinary; but only if we have eyes to see.

A true transformation of consciousness allows us to see reality as it really is, before we start shaping it with our calculating minds. We begin to live from a different place; a more spacious and forgiving place. We learn to see the hidden beauty in all things and especially in people. Our judging mind becomes a compassionate mind. It is not that we no longer make judgements. We make them from a different source, not from the narrow perspective of the ego, but from the broad expanse of the soul which has come alive to the God within.

The marginalisation of the contemplative tradition in recent centuries has cut us off from our mystical identity. We have reduced mysticism to an extraordinary way, full of strange visions or experiences, certainly not part of the mainstream. In fact we are all created for mysticism, for union with God, for union with all reality. Karl Rahner described it as *the ordinary vocation of the Christian.*

Mysticism gives us direct access to who we are in God. We move from ideas about God to a direct experience of God. It is this desire and hunger for direct experience of God which is at the heart of the world's hunger today. This has to be personally experienced. It cannot really be taught. As Thomas Merton says, *the tragedy is that we don't realise that we are always in union with God and with everyone else.* It is the way of wisdom that all great religions teach. The document on the Church in The Second Vatican Council proclaimed that all priests should abound in contemplation so that they can lead the people into true joy. If only that were the case what a different Church we would have. The good news is that it is beginning to happen.

What is really interesting is that this change is not just occurring in religious circles but right across humanity and it represents:

a movement away from ideas and institutions that embrace material values, reductionism, hierarchical control, and the supremacy of the personal ego towards a new paradigm that embraces spiritual values, wholeness, integration, cooperation, and the interrelationship of all human beings regardless of their differences—indeed the interrelationship of all elements of the universe itself.[7]

I think that the mystics would all say *Amen* to that.

---

[7] Edmund J Bourne, *Global Shift* (New Harbinger Publications, Inc Oakland, CA 2008) p65

Chapter 3 — Re-Enchantment

When you regain sense of your life as a journey of discovery, you return to rhythm with yourself. When you take the time to travel with reverence a richer life unfolds before you. Moments of beauty begin to upbraid your days. When your mind becomes more acquainted with reverence, the light, grace, and elegance of beauty find you more frequently.[8]

One of the most damaging perceptions of the lives of holy people and mystics is that they are detached from the world and from people. Would you want to invite the mystics to a meal, share a glass of wine with them, or have a pint in a pub? Personally I would find it fascinating, but I imagine I am in a minority. One of my great regrets about the gospels is that Jesus is never recorded as sharing laughter with his friends. I once expressed this regret to a renowned scripture scholar and he reminded me that Jesus didn't write the gospels himself. There is no doubt that Jesus is frequently described as eating and drinking with the wrong people. The rather serious Pharisees and Scribes are shocked at this behaviour and Jesus himself throws back, in their faces, the accusation that he is a glutton and a drunkard.[9]

We proclaim that God is unconditional and infinite love. We teach that Jesus became fully human and shared everything about our human condition, apart from sin. Yet we still struggle to believe in the reality of the Incarnation. Over the centuries, we Christians have tended to split the world into sacred and secular. We have identified certain places (e.g. churches) as holy and certain people (priests and religious) as holy and the Church has tended to reinforce that view. Even the word *clergy* means the separated ones.

---

8 John O'Donohue, *Divine Beauty* (Bantam Press, London 2003) p28
9 Matthew 11:18-19

I often think that the Holy Spirit is using the vocations crisis in the Western Church to force us to take seriously the gifts of the laity, recognising the foundational importance of baptism.

This split in the understanding of the word *holy* is another aspect of the prevailing mindset of dualism. The mystics don't have this problem. Their realised sense of oneness gives them new eyes with which to look out at reality, and contemplation is precisely that—a loving look at reality. The shift is from egocentric seeing to a non-dual unified sense of awareness. The practice of contemplative prayer, on a regular basis, provides us with new software. The calculating mind tries to split reality; the contemplative mind sees the underlying unity. Contemplation is not just a way of praying; it is a new way of seeing.

As infinite love, God is continually inviting us to see the essential beauty of all things. As infinite love, God is offering us a taste of the joy of a life lived not in the isolation of autonomous existence, but in union with the gracious source of all Being. Our eyes are gradually opened to see this holy mystery in all creation. The infinite transcendence of God's loving presence invades our moments of awareness. This is the joy that Jesus promises his followers, his own joy which he shares in communion with the Father and is given to us in the Spirit. This is why Thomas Merton is able to describe contemplative living as *the fullness of life*.

In his book *Seeds of Contemplation* Merton has a chapter headed, *Everything that is, is Holy*. This is a crucial insight for the mystics who can teach our rather knowing and cynical culture how to re-enchant the world and recover its intrinsic holiness. The Church also needs to learn this message and reframe holiness not as detachment from life but a very real attachment to and celebration of the God-given nature of reality. As Merton points out, I only have to be detached from egotistic ways, from the false self, from seeing everything from my own limited perspective:

> It is not true that the saints and the great contemplatives never loved created things, and had no understanding and appreciation of the

world, with its sights and sounds and the people living in it. They loved everything and everyone.[10]

The whole purpose of Jesus becoming human is to heal the split between heaven and earth, between sacred and secular, the invisible and the visible. He teaches us how to combine the universal and the particular, the eternal *now* with *this particular moment*, the power of God with the vulnerability and fragility of the human. He reveals the underlying unity between matter and spirit together and asks us not to separate them. Sadly, and all too often, our dualistic minds keep splitting them.

Reading the gospels, it appears that Jesus doesn't spend a lot of time in holy places such as the synagogue, although he does visit them. When the evangelists describe Jesus at prayer, it is usually in nature, in the wide open spaces:

In the morning, while it was still very dark, he got up and went out to a deserted place, and there he prayed.[11]

Immediately he made his disciples get into the boat and go on ahead to the other side, to Bethsaida, while he dismissed the crowd. After saying farewell to them, he went up on the mountain to pray.[12]

At daybreak he departed and went into a deserted place.[13]

The pattern is clear and it confirms the experience of many people. When we can withdraw a little from the busyness of life—and that isn't always easy in our driven culture—we can get a taste of contemplative awareness. These moments are always being given to us as part of the God-given nature of reality that surrounds us, but without an inner life

---

10 Thomas Merton, *New Seeds of Contemplation* (New Directions , NY 1972) p22
11 Mark 1:35
12 Mark 6:45-46
13 Luke 4:42

it is difficult to be truly present. So God gives us all kinds of clues to awaken us to the infinite grace and beauty of life.

The example of Jesus points to nature as one of the privileged arenas where these experiences arise, where the holy mystery becomes more apparent. Places of natural beauty clearly lend themselves to this kind of contemplative seeing. I live in an urban environment but not too far from Crosby Beach where the Mersey estuary meets the Irish Sea. It is a wonderful place to walk and take in the beauty of the ocean, the Welsh hills in the background, and the 100 life-size statues on the sandy beach placed there by the artist Antony Gormley. It is easy to get a glimpse of God's beauty in a place like that. What is more important, perhaps, is being present to the holy mystery in ordinary everyday experiences. The mystics teach us to open ourselves to the eternal now, the *thisness* of a particular moment which for us is always passing, and reminds us of the cosmic dance in which we all share. Such moments of contemplative awareness are given to us constantly and witness to the holiness of all reality. These moments reveal the mystery of Being, in which we all participate.

Today the scientists are telling us that we live in a continuously evolving universe, although it is more accurate to say that we don't really live in the universe: we are part of the process. We are the conscious part of the process of becoming which began for us in the Big Bang, 13.7 billion years ago. The old idea that we could dominate the earth and use it for our own selfish ends is being replaced by the realisation that we share the gift of being with everything that has been created. Reverence and respect is replacing exploitation and greed. The mystics have long taught that the universe is full of mystery and alive with the creative energy and love of God. Instead of exploiting the planet from a position of dominance, we are recognising that we are just a small part of the total mystery. Our dignity, as human beings, is that we are the conscious part, but it requires a new humility as we marvel at the wonders that the scientists are regularly revealing about the majesty and the splendour of endless galaxies and stars. Our own bodies are indeed stardust as we celebrate our unity with all creation. Centuries ago, that great mystic, Francis of Assisi was speaking about *Brother Sun* and *Sister Moon*. Today, with Francis, we are learning to re-enchant creation as the scientists share insights with the poets and the mystics.

The sense of oneness with nature flows into a sense of oneness with others and flows directly from our oneness with God. Our Western culture has placed individuality above everything. But it is an individuality that has cut us off from our roots. We haven't seen ourselves as connected with the world we have chosen to exploit. It is an isolated individuality. We tend to over-identify what differentiates ourselves from others rather than what unites us and many have cut themselves off from God by embracing atheism or agnosticism. By losing its mystical tradition the Church, too, sought its identity in being Catholic or Christian rather than human.

We preferred to live inside our boundaries rather than move beyond them, as Jesus did. This puts too much pressure on us to create our own meaning and significance. In the secular world it is all down to achievement and effort, material success and reputation. Being successful in a world of scarcity means that *I have to have more than you have* in order to feel my worth and significance. Even in the Church we have reduced the spiritual journey largely to effort and willpower—*the more I can do for God the more he will be pleased with me.*

The spiritual consciousness, breaking out today, seeks to recover the original vision of Jesus rooted in the mystery of the Incarnation. It is a radically different starting point, one that doesn't separate us from others but unites us in our common humanity. Jesus speaks about the mystery of the kingdom as the pearl of great price. The mystics tell us that we are the pearl of great price; not by anything we do, but by being in fundamental relationship with Jesus who assumes our humanity. He is the true pearl in the Father's eyes and through the gift of the Spirit we too are pearls in the eyes of God. Our worth and value is in fact infinite, because it doesn't come from us, but is pure gift. The Franciscan theologian Blessed Duns Scotus used the word *haeceity* to describe the wonderful mystery of who we are in God. *Haeceity* means *thisness*. We all possess it in a different way. None of us is identical to another, as even twins will testify. We reflect our *thisness* our uniqueness, our individuality and at the same time see and honour and reverence the *thisness* of everyone else.

What happens to Jesus in the Incarnation is what happens inside of us. In Jesus the Universal Mystery (God) became visible in his concrete individual humanity. The mystics remind us that we are not human beings trying to reach God but we are all united to him in the deepest possible way. We are spiritual beings who have to discover and not jettison our humanity. The challenge of spiritual maturity is to accept ourselves with our strengths and weaknesses, and all we are asked to do is to offer that back to God, safe in the knowledge that God accepts all that we are.

The awareness of the divine within is *the pearl of great price, the treasure hidden in a field*. Eckhart Tolle reminds us that we are who we are because we share in the gift of God's own life and love. Because the word *God* tends to be colonised by different faiths he uses the word *Being*:

> Being is the eternal ever-present One Life beyond the myriad forms of life that are subject to birth and death. However Being is not only beyond but also deep within every form as its innermost invisible and indestructible essence. This means that it is accessible to you now, as your own deepest self, your true nature. But don't seek to grasp it with your mind. Don't try to understand it. You can know it only when the mind is still. When you are present, when your attention is fully and intensely in the Now, Being can be felt, but it can never be understood mentally. To regain awareness of Being and to abide in that state of *feeling-realization* is enlightenment.[14]

---

14 Eckhart Tolle *The Power of Now* (Hodder & Stoughton London 2005) p10

What Tolle means by *enlightenment* is what we Christians call *salvation*. It is a foundational experience that is offered to everyone, but it has to be individually received. Once it is experienced, not intellectually by the mind, but with the more intuitive kind of knowing, at the level of soul, then it provides all our needs for security and significance. We are who we are because we have received the gift, and it becomes our task to live from the enchanted centre within to reach out to re-enchant the whole of creation.

This kind of intuitive knowing is not something that we can grasp for ourselves. We don't need to grasp it; it is already there, but it is buried like the treasure in the field. The spiritual journey is therefore, an awakening, a becoming present to the treasure within. Once we discover it within ourselves we are then able to see it within others and within the whole of creation. We are not talking pantheism here; we are not God. But we do participate in all our concrete thisness and particularity in the Being of God. The love of God is given to us in every moment with extravagance and abundance. It would break open our hearts if we could be fully aware of it. It is what I caught a glimpse of in the dying heart of baby Damien.

Chapter 4 — Recovering the Sacred

We have lost something. What is it? A sense of the sacred. Why is the sacred important? The sacred is important for human freedom because *the sacred* signifies that which cannot be bought or sold. The hope for the world lies in recovering its sacred identity. The sacred, in the end, won't be controlled or manipulated and certainly cannot be co-opted by the consumer culture. It is the guarantor of true freedom.[15]

Moments of what might be called spontaneous contemplative experience reveal the true nature of reality. Instead of seeing the world as a neutral environment, we begin to open ourselves to the inherent holiness of all things. The new consciousness, sought by increasing numbers today, finds a home in sacred space. From the beginning of time, human beings have been aware of a mysterious presence, the sense of the sacred. All religions have taught this and invited their followers to taste and see. In our everyday lives we experience it not just in nature but in everything around us, if we have eyes to see. The task of mature religion is to invite us to become more aware of, and present to, this mystery; not just in ecstatic moments, but in the experience of the ordinary.

James Finlay relates an interesting story during the time when he was a novice with Thomas Merton in Gethsemane Monastery, Kentucky. He asked Merton if he would become his spiritual director. Merton agreed, but only on one condition. At that time Finlay took care of the monastery pig farm. Merton insisted that when he came to see him he could only speak about one topic. He told Finlay only to talk to him about the pigs. This might seem strange advice from a world-renowned spiritual guide and teacher but the point he was making was that if Finlay could be fully present to the pigs he would be more in tune with the presence of God in so many other areas. We think presence is easy

---

15 Dean Alan Jones. See http://deanalanjones.com/

but in our world of multi-tasking it seems to becoming more difficult for us. When travelling into Liverpool I sometimes take the train. I am usually surrounded by fellow passengers, especially the younger ones, glued to their iPods and clutching their phones with heads down, scanning anxiously for emails or text messages. It is not as if there is anything wrong with this, but it does give us an indication of how difficult we find it to be present. Our Western culture is dominated by noise and external stimulus.

Centuries ago, monasteries were set up to try to answer this need for the discipline of presence. For those of us who live in the world we do not have this luxury, which is probably one reason why active religious orders did not teach the path of contemplation. The laity, too, were never encouraged to tread this path to awareness. The secular world and culture seem to almost actively undermine any sense of the sacred. Many modern successful people are too embarrassed to admit any religious dimension in their lives. The most obvious signs of religious belief—if you can call it that—are exhibited on the football fields as players routinely cross themselves or point heavenwards when they score a goal. I'm not quite sure how God deals with all these claims to his support and intervention; although I have a sneaking feeling he remains a secret fan of Bolton Wanderers![16]

What is worthy of note are genuine signs of spiritual hunger in our contemporary world. David Tacey, in his book *The Spirituality Revolution,* refers to an insightful essay written by a nineteen-year-old student, Elizabeth, for one of his courses on spirituality at La Trobe University, Melbourne, Australia. After leaving behind her childhood faith, Elizabeth describes her struggles to feel at home in the secular climate of today; but the effort leaves her feeling superficial and fragmented. She wanted to reconnect with a deeper life within her but was unsure how to proceed. She clearly identifies the problem:

> I was scared to acknowledge the sacred in case it meant the ultimate death of the subtle underlying apathy that protected myself and all

16 The premiership football team I support.

of us, from the shocking reality of the presence of mystery in our lives.[17]

I think that Elizabeth is identifying a root problem many of us have in the face of mystery, a problem that affects openly religious people, even religious professionals such as the clergy and religious, as well as sceptics: the need for control over our lives. To be in control is the mark of a sophisticated mature adult. The problem is, as spiritual teachers in all the great religions tell us—that in the face of mystery, control has to be surrendered.

In the first chapter I described how immature religious teaching wants to keep us under control, and sadly, we too often easily acquiesce to that condition. The Catholic Church has long been a practitioner of control, stressing obedience and conformity. Sadly this produces an immature faith. Mature religion should lead us into mystery and this is precisely the challenge and the great summons to religion today: to rediscover the sense of mystery, the sense of the sacred, at the heart of all reality. Having identified her resistance, Elizabeth goes on to describe the challenging nature of surrendering to mystery:

> In these sentences I have revealed something which is extremely difficult and confronting to admit. I realise I do believe in an *Other*, in a sacred other. If I analyse my feelings thoroughly, I would probably conclude that it was God. The reason I put God on hold was because it was easier to live in the distractions of the secular without commitment or responsibility towards the sacred. To make that conscious choice is to admit my own weaknesses and frailty as a human being among other human beings like me. It is to admit my dependence on a mystery and beauty greater than myself.[18]

---

17 Quoted in David Tacey, *The Spirituality Revolution* (Brunner-Routledge, UK 2004) p117
18 Quoted in David Tacey, *The Spirituality Revolution* (Brunner-Routledge UK 2004) p119

What Elizabeth honestly identifies in herself is true to some degree of all of us. It harks right back to that brilliant mythical account of *The Fall* in Genesis. Adam and Eve enjoyed a serene relationship with God, but they were seduced by the serpent's offer to become their own gods. By challenging their dependency on God they would not only take control of their own lives, but they would gain knowledge of good and evil. This could almost be called the emerging of the egocentric mind, which lives by comparing and judging: who is right and who is wrong, who is in and who is out, who is up and who is down.

What Elizabeth identifies as a current issue is as old as the hills. In the past the egocentric mindset—which Jesus challenges us to change—as set inside a culture and consciousness, saw itself inside the sacred. However they lived, people were naturally believers in something greater than themselves. Today, that faith culture has collapsed in the face of the explosion of the scientific reasoning that created our modern world with all its incredible achievements. The myths of religion were replaced by the myths of reason. But those rational myths are now showing signs of decline, as we see a world riven by violence, war, poverty, crime, and environmental crises.

The turning by reflective people, typified by Elizabeth, is not back to religion with its dogmas and doctrines, but to a deeper opening to a sense of the sacred, of a mystery that is both beyond yet strangely compelling. It is distant and elusive yet it seems to be at home in us at the same time. Part of the reason that reflective people are not turning to organised religion is because many of us, inside that tradition, have lost our mystical roots. We don't know how to guide people in a compelling way to a recovery of the sense of the sacred. The louder voices in this field within Churches are often identified with deeply conservative positions. They are at ease in the father-knows-best attitude of pre-Second Vatican Council theology and the restoration of traditional liturgical rites.

We need to reconnect the call of the sacred with true and authentic human flourishing, to show how the sacred penetrates every aspect of our existence. We need to live lives that are not afraid to see the whole of our humanity transformed in the mystery of love. We have to recapture and celebrate the experience of the good news that Jesus came to reveal. If we can take our lives out of our moral straightjackets we need not be afraid of the weaknesses and frailty that Elizabeth found in herself. Jesus did not come for the virtuous and the perfect; he came to invite weak and vulnerable people to grow into his forgiving and incredibly creative love. Our lives can then be led into the joy of kingdom consciousness as we allow our hearts to reach out in service to others. The Incarnation assures us that the divine is found in ordinary flesh and blood.

If we can move beyond the dualistic judgements of the ego we can reconnect not just with the sacred in ourselves but in others and in everything around us. An authentic and mature spiritual life is much more about mysticism than moralism.

We begin to see, with new eyes, the glory of God that is available, everywhere. I remember drinking coffee in a Liverpool café recently when I became vividly aware of and present to the volume of love being poured out in front of me, as an elderly wife helped her handicapped husband to a seat, as a mother fed her baby with patience and love, as an attractive young girl shared her thoughts with her friend, as young children ran playfully around their parents. I was looking at the extraordinary in the ordinary; the inherent holiness of all life.

If we are prepared to give up the control needs of our ego we can surrender more often to the holy mystery that is life. For Thomas Merton contemplation is life itself, fully aware that it is alive:

> It is spontaneous awe at the sacredness of life, of being. It is gratitude for life, for awareness and for being. It is a vivid realisation of the fact that life and being in us proceed from an invisible, transcendent and infinitely abundant Source. Contemplation is, above all, awareness of the reality of that Source. It **knows** the Source

> obscurely, inexplicably, but with a certitude that
> goes beyond reason and simple faith.[19]

Merton's combining of the words *obscurely* and *certitude* to describe contemplation gives us important clues to the paradox at the heart of the mystical journey, which we will explore more in a later chapter. We can all experience moments of contemplative awareness in nature or in moments of intimacy with those we love, and in the everyday reality of what is. We learn to look with the eyes of the poet and the artist.

We have seen how Jesus retired often to the hills to pray, and he also celebrated friendship in relaxed meals with his disciples and friends such as Martha, Mary and Lazarus. There can be many moments of graced awakening that give us the taste of non-duality, when we sense the unity at the heart of all things. They reveal to us our true identity in God as opposed to the dualistic secular way of looking at reality which finds it difficult to get beyond the externals such as skin colour, nationality, status, achievements, and opinions. In these moments we are fully alive as Merton says, rooted in the graced conviction that we are precious and holy in God's eyes.

But it is only a taste because these graced moments pass and we return to our customary state of unawareness of the sacred. That unawareness, however, is now different, because we now realise that we are unaware. This subtle sense is what Merton means when he describes contemplative experience as obscure knowledge. The mystics describe this kind of knowing as *unknowing*. The classic title *The Cloud of Unknowing*, written by an anonymous English monk in the fourteenth century, captures the paradox at the heart of contemplation. It is never perfect vision; nevertheless it awakens us to what Merton describes as a certitude that goes beyond reason and simple faith. At a deep visceral level in our souls we have been awakened to the sacred source of all reality. A *metanoia*, a radical change of outlook, has occurred that changes how we see, think and

---

19 Thomas Merton *New Seeds of Contemplation* (New Directions Paperback NY 1972) p1

feel. Even when the experience fades we still sense a longing and an ache in the depths of our being.

This is part of the wounding that occurs in contemplative experience. In one of his poems St John of the Cross says that as we go on our journey through life God follows us like a hart, a small deer. At some point he springs out and wounds us before dashing away. That is a wound of love, and the hart continues to follow us and wound us again and again in the same place, in the place of deepest hurt. This seems to us to be unfair, yet it opens us to the essential vulnerability of love. Despite the ache, we begin to sense that there is no other way for us to live. The powerful myth of *The Fall* says that we are all in exile, longing to return to the unitive experience of *The Garden of Eden*.

I think that when Elizabeth was reflecting on her experience of something lost, of a need to be present to the sacred mystery of things she was articulating something of this woundedness. It is a kind of homesickness and even though we set out to numb the pain—and our culture has so many ways of inviting us to do this—it never goes away. It is the Spirit calling us home.

In recent years a number of labyrinths have appeared in churches and retreat centres. They reflect the ins and outs of the spiritual journey that rarely takes a straight path. As you walk the labyrinth you are led both towards and away from the centre. This pattern is deliberate and teaches us that the path of the journey has it twists and turns and the consoling truth is that God uses every aspect of our journey. When you reach the centre you are invited to stand and simply become alert and open to whatever the Spirit is saying. I recall walking the labyrinth in Grace Cathedral, San Francisco. The message at the centre was very clear; *take me home.*

The journey is really a journey back to our true centre, but it is not without difficulties and challenges. We have to be prepared to move out of our comfort zones, and to confront some less appealing aspects of our personalities. Our secular culture doesn't encourage us to walk the spiritual journey, and even institutional religion prefers to keep us at the level of answers rather than difficult questions. Maybe that is why Jesus says that we have to be prepared to enter the narrow gate.

Many genuine searchers today, like Elizabeth, choose spirituality rather than organised religion. Karl Rahner famously said that Christians of the 21st century will have to embrace mysticism or else we will simply cease to exist. Despite renewed interest in the sacred, the numbers attending churches in the Western world continue to decline. The challenge is clear. We have to lead people home; but we cannot do that unless we too have travelled the sacred path.

Chapter 5 — Who are you?

**On that day you will know that I am in my Father
and you in me and I in you.**[20]

Becoming more aware of the holy mystery which surrounds us at
all times, with infinite love, involves becoming more aware of
who we really are. It is clear that Jesus identified with the
wisdom teaching that all human beings suffer from a case of mistaken
identity. This is very counter-intuitive for our Western culture that
places so much emphasis on individuality—the *I did it my way*
mentality that is so highly prized in our world today. In fact the attempt
to carve out a distinctive and personal identity seems to be the whole
point and purpose of life, and it is often couched in a rather selfish
That's the way I am, take it or leave it approach.

Spiritual teachers have for centuries warned against this warped
understanding of the identity question. The problem is that the private
individual self is too small a container to carry the mystery of who we
really are. It centres on my point of view, my ideas, my judgements, my
emotions, my opinions. It is focussed on my busy little self with its own
agenda and limited point of view. It tends to see others as threats and
dangers and is largely built on the shifting sands of anxiety and fear.
This fear can sometimes escalate to aggressive and even violent
behaviour, and a negative regard for the stranger, and anyone who is
different.

Spiritual teachers call this *the false self*, or *the small self*. Jesus warns
against this small self getting in the way of the liberating journey to the
true self. He says that whoever wants to protect this small or false self,
will lose his real life, and the one who is willing to lose it will truly
discover the real thing. The language he uses is strong and challenging,
speaking of the need to die to this small self. But this tension between
the small or false self and the larger or true self goes to the heart of the
spiritual journey. Getting in touch with the true self is the gateway

---

20 John 14:20

to the fullness of life that Jesus comes to reveal. It is what he speaks about to the Samaritan woman he meets at the well.[21] She has come to get ordinary water but Jesus invites her to taste a different kind of water, living water that springs up inside her. If she drinks this water she will never thirst again. These words echo Jesus' invitation to his disciples to pray by going into their inner room, closing the door and meeting the Father who awaits them in secret.[22] What does he mean by this inner room?

We all have what might be called ordinary consciousness. This is our everyday awareness of what we see, touch, smell, taste, and hear. It is the gift of self-reflexive consciousness, the awareness of myself as a separate being, with my particular ideas, assumptions, gifts, points of view and emotional reactions to life. This is what we understand to be our identity. It tends to be defensive and wary of threats to our well-being and reputation. It sees everything in terms of the subject/object polarity. This is our thinking mind, and it is largely controlled by the ego. If we were to really examine it we would find it is our thinking mind which keeps us locked into the dualistic way of seeing and judging, which is why all mature religions teach us to go beyond the ego to a deeper place. For this to happen we need to switch our minds off by a deliberate choice of silence. This is what Jesus means by *go to your inner room and close the door*; he wants us to get out of our ordinary awareness, or what might be called the egoic mind, or the calculating mind. It is a move to spiritual awareness or spiritual consciousness.

At this deeper level we discover that we do not have to be dominated by our thoughts. Thoughts include feelings as well as concepts and ideas, all our perceptions in fact. At the level of our spiritual consciousness we learn that although we have thoughts and feelings we are *not* our thoughts and feelings. We learn the vital element of distancing ourselves from what is going on at the superficial or ordinary level of consciousness. This is a major step in the spiritual journey and

---

21 John 4
22 Matthew 6

is the reason why mature religion always demands some form of regular practice to keep us from slipping back into our dualistic point of view. Mature religion is more concerned about *how we see* rather than which ideas we believe in. This is the kind of faith that Jesus constantly speaks about. Do we trust that the mystery that surrounds us is fundamentally and foundationally a loving and gracious mystery?

The word that Jesus uses for encountering and tasting the holy mystery that surrounds us is *prayer*. Not prayer in the sense of saying prayers, or trying to get something from God, a kind of prayer that can still keep the ego in control, but prayer as surrendering to the mystery. Our rational minds tend to resist this kind of movement, as we seek to explain everything. In fact the word *mystery* doesn't mean something that cannot be known. It refers to something that is infinitely knowable. It is a knowing that in the Christian tradition becomes intensely personal:

> The essential religious experience is that you are being *known through* more than knowing anything particular yourself. Yet despite this difference it will feel like true knowing....At this point, God becomes more of a verb than a noun, more a process than a conclusion, more an experience than a dogma, more a personal relationship than an idea. There is someone dancing with you and you are not afraid of making mistakes.[23]

The problem is that most religious believers are not in touch with this deeper level of spiritual awareness. Maybe we experience some spontaneous moments of contemplative awareness as we gaze at the setting sun, or see the face of a child, or see the beauty of the autumn leaves, but these moments are fleeting and rare. Our religious training has set us on a path of behaviour rather than initiate us into a whole new way of seeing. Too many religious believers appear judgemental and quite narrow-minded. We seem to believe in a God who will reward the good and punish the bad, a God who prefers the kind of

---

23 Richard Rohr *The Naked Now* (The Crossroad Publishing Company NY 2009) p23

people that we like and approve of. It is not surprising that this kind of religion has created the levels of atheism, anger and hostility that we see in the West. In recent centuries the Church has rarely taught anything about the contemplative tradition. Mysticism has been viewed as rather odd, and certainly not mainstream; but without some form of practice of silent prayer we cannot really free ourselves from dualistic minds. The mystic character encourages us to try to accept people as they are, rather than fit them into the bias our own point of view. This is not easy, and it is one reason why the contemplative way of seeing is so much needed in our fragmented world in which we all too quickly rush to judgement. Much of our fragmented world, especially in its religious aspects, finds itself caught in this trap.

If ordinary consciousness leaves us largely trapped in our egos, spiritual consciousness gives us a whole new way of seeing and perceiving reality. Instead of being anxious and defensive, spiritual awareness opens us to the divine image in others. We begin to sense this because we are now in touch with the divine image within ourselves. We begin to draw our life from a different source. We move from the separateness of the dualistic mind to the unitive non-dual seeing of the contemplative mind. This is the *water* rising up from within that Jesus awakened in the Samaritan woman. The more we experience this awareness the more it begins to influence our ordinary level of awareness. Our rational mind starts to expand and instead of narrowing down our perception it begins to be more open to the mystery of the other. St Augustine calls it seeing with the eye of the heart and he says this is the goal of Christian life for everybody.

This new kind of seeing arises from a different sense of identity. Instead of seeing ourselves in isolation and separateness we move to a more intuitive understanding of our essential relatedness to others and to creation. This is non-dual awareness and it connects us with the Great Mystery of love, compassion, forgiveness and inclusion that we call God. Our life and work is then more integrated as we continue to draw from the mysterious source within that we call the Holy Spirit.

Jesus highlights the need to harmonise our ordinary and our spiritual consciousness in the story of Martha and Mary.[24] While Mary sits at the feet of Jesus totally absorbed in his presence, Martha is preparing the meal. Nothing wrong with that of course, but this is a story about *presence* and Martha is too wrapped up in her small self to be fully present. She is so stressed and anxious that she gets judgemental about her sister's lack of help. She even tells Jesus what he should be doing: pointing out Mary's faults! Jesus reassures her that only one thing really matters. It is not Martha's activity that is the problem; it is the fact that her work is not truly centred. Wrapped up in her small self rather than her true self, she is not able to be truly present to her work and so not truly present either to her sister or to Jesus.

Mary has reached a stage of deeper integration. She knows how to be present because she knows that authentic activity always flows from a deeper source. I know, in my own case, how often I think that the spiritual progress can be achieved by my willpower and my effort. In contrast, Mary teaches us that it is much more a matter of willingness, of surrender to the flow of love—that is the divine indwelling. That, for Jesus, is the one thing that really matters. It marks the shift from ego consciousness to Christ consciousness. This is another defeat for the ego since I like to think that I am in charge and control of my spiritual life. By contrast, all that matters, if I can embrace *the mystery within*, is to surrender to the love that is always flowing from deep within me. We cannot initiate this love; we are only asked to surrender. Once again we meet the invitation to *die* to the ego's desire to be in control, so that we can live in union with the Great Love, the Great Compassion.

The Martha/Mary story is a classic spiritual *both/and* story. It is always a question of integration so that our ordinary level of awareness does not close off the deeper life within. Both levels of awareness need to be aligned to the third level of awareness which is the presence of God in the core of our being. Our activity can then be purified of any selfish motivation so that we are no longer dependent on success or approval. We can move beyond the incessant cry of the ego: *I need, I want* or

---

24 Luke 10:38-41

Pay attention to me. This is not easy but it can be incredibly liberating and lead to a much more joyful and peaceful life. It is not something we can achieve; it is a gift that we learn to receive, through prayer.

Jesus famously told the inquiring Pharisee, Nicodemus, that he had to be born again to experience this new kind of life, born of water and the Spirit. This happens, of course, at our baptism. But for many of us the gifts of the Spirit remain dormant. The Early Church went to great lengths to demonstrate what really happens at baptism as they practised total immersion. As infant baptism became the norm this was reduced to pouring a little water over the head of the child: hardly the most dramatic symbolism of a death leading to a new life. Baptism, in fact, has become the great sacrament of belonging, but it means much more than this. It should initiate us into this different form of life, as we move beyond the limited horizons of the small self and enter more fully into our new identity as children of God.

This journey is not an easy one, and it cannot be done without surrendering control. Although each one of us is unique, in our individuality, we are not in control of the mystery of our being. We cannot construct our identity as an independent project. That is the problem of the false self. Our identity can only be found in the unfolding of a relationship with *An Other, An Absolute.* That is the truth that Adam and Eve rejected.

Imagine yourself standing in front of a mirror, and your image reflected perfectly before you is able to speak. Your image tells you that you are no longer needed. He/she can exist without you. You only have to move to the edge of the mirror for the image to start to disappear! That is the way we depend totally on God for our existence and identity. This is not a constriction on our freedom because as God's image we are able to reflect the holy mystery of love that is given to us, to delight in and to share with others. We are created as images of God and outside of God we are just an illusion.

Inside of God we have everything. That is why Jesus speaks the language of paradox in his most sublime teachings. The poor, the gentle, the non-violent, the merciful, those in other words who know how to receive, are given more and more of the abundant gift that is life, the living water welling up within us.

This is the life that the mystics discover and invite us to share. To be loved and accepted and forgiven by the Great Compassion that is God is to know the meaning of the word *salvation*. Instead of having to construct and build our own identity, worth and significance through willpower and striving, that entire burden is lifted from us. In Mary's words all we have to say is, *Let it be*. All the effort to get it right and be successful and perfect can be abandoned by a simple movement of surrender to the holy mystery. We move from willpower to willingness.

This mystery, for us Christians, is a living person, someone we can relate to and fall in love with. By uniting humanity and Godhead Jesus shows us how to put it all together, how to overcome the great split, the great divide between God and Man. Adam and Eve thought that they could become their own gods by grasping the fruit of the tree of the knowledge of good and evil. Jesus comes to reassure us that it is God who wants to be united with us. He invites us into non-dual living, to share with him in his reconciling mission to bring everything together in unity. We pray at every Mass that all cosmic opposites can be reconciled in him, through him, and with him.

The dualistic mind gets us started in life and it can achieve many useful things, but in the great journey of life's meaning and significance, it blocks the way. It is too small and restrictive. We long for freedom and yet we live in bondage to the small self:

> There is only one problem on which all my existence, my peace and my happiness depend: to discover myself in discovering God. If I find him I will find myself and if I find my true self I will find him...This is something that no man can ever do alone.....the only one who can teach me to find God is God, himself, Alone.[25]

25 Thomas Merton *New Seeds of Contemplation* (New Directions Publishing Co NY 1972) p36

Jesus tells us to change our mindset; Paul tells us to put on the mind of Christ. Then we begin to understand why the mystics speak the language of realised oneness with God and realised oneness with everything else.

Chapter 6 — The Way of Paradox

We aren't focussed on the great mystery. Rather religion has tended to create people who think they have God in their pockets, people with quick, easy, glib answers. That's why so much of the West is understandingly abandoning religion. People know the great mystery cannot be that simple and facile. If the great mystery is indeed the Great Mystery, it will lead into paradox, into darkness, into journeys that never cease. That is what prayer is about.[26]

Whenever we travel to new places we like to talk to someone who has been there before us. What is it like, and especially, for English people, what is the weather like? In the spiritual journey into the infinite mystery that surrounds us we also need guides, those who have travelled the path before us and can lessen our fears and anxieties. As the hunger for direct experience of God grows in our world, more and more people are getting to know the mystics, whose wisdom has been largely forgotten in the Western Church. Happily, things are changing. I was being driven to the airport in Malta recently by a young Salesian Brother. He was asking about some of the things I had shared in a retreat reflection the previous day. We got into a discussion about John of the Cross and were so taken up by this that we missed the airport entrance! I recall once listening to a tape on contemplative prayer in my car when I drove through two sets of red lights in Liverpool city centre. Not to be recommended—we need our calculating rational minds in our daily routines.

Reflecting on my conversation with the young Salesian Brother, I was so impressed with his interest in the great Spanish mystics. I don't remember being invited to read about John of the Cross in my years of formation. In fact I remember an elderly Salesian priest dismissing John of the Cross by quoting his famous dictum *nada, nada, nada, nothing, nothing, nothing*. What on earth does that mean, he asked?

---

26 Richard Rohr *Everything Belongs* (Crossroad Publishing Co NY 2003) p35

I am certainly no expert on John of the Cross but I have begun to understand the importance, the crucial importance, of paradox in the spiritual journey. For John, *nothing* meant *everything*.

The mystics all agree that if we are faithful to our spiritual practice we begin to experience a new desire and capacity for love. An interesting and challenging aspect of the gospels is the fact that Jesus commands us to love. This strikes our contemporary understanding of love as strange. How can you command someone to love? Our Western world looks askance at arranged marriages; for us marriage has to be a personal free choice after an experience of falling in love. What I think Jesus is getting at is that for true and lasting happiness we have to move beyond the personal agenda of who we like and dislike with its focus on my needs, my point of view. We have to learn to go beyond the need for positive strokes and constant affirmation and go out to meet the needs of others. That tends to be the agenda for the first half of life. The second half of life begins when we grow beyond this small self. This is the *agape*[27] love of Jesus which reaches out to the other. The more we give ourselves away, the more we become who we truly are.

Jesus doesn't say wait until you have dealt with all your wounds and needs for healing; he says go out and do it now. This is where contemplation and action come together. God chooses to heal us at a deep level of our being in contemplative moments of prayer. There we learn our true identity, who we are in God, before we have achieved or done anything. It is a moment of what we call biblical knowing, when we are *known through and through,* in the deepest sense. That knowing brings about an enlargement of who we are, it gives us a new identity, we realise that we are not isolated individuals having to defend our own limited space in the world. When we touch our deepest being we touch the Being of God. We discover that God is Being-in-Love. The mystical path, the path within, becomes the path of love, the path without.

---

27 Three words have traditionally been used to describe love: *eros, philia* and *agape. Eros* refers to desire-love and includes sexual love, *philia* to friendship-love, and *agape* to divine-love.

For the mystics this knowledge is not just theoretical head knowledge; it is a lived experience. Back in the fourteenth century, an anonymous English monk was guiding a young searcher for God. In the classic work known as *The Cloud of Unknowing.* He explained to the young man that this yearning for a deeper and fuller life wasn't coming from himself, but was a response to what he called a *blind stirring of love.* It is pure gift, pure grace, it is what John of the Cross called *the wound of love.* It is what the Russian writer of *The Way of the Pilgrim* called *an unappeasable desire.* It is worth noting that the mystical traditions of Hinduism and Buddhism record the same felt conviction. It is an experience of a gift from beyond the self.

This gift is so delicate and fragile that it can easily be extinguished by the highly extroverted and noisy world we live in. The Old Testament describes it as *a gentle breeze*; the New Testament calls it *the pearl of great price.* If one is faithful to its prompting, the desire grows to create space and silence, to enter the inner room, and there to learn to sit in loving presence and awareness of this mystery. In the early stages of this allurement, God often rewards the searching soul with consolations and a deepening conviction of being loved un-conditionally. This will not last because the wound of love just gets deeper. We get emptied in order to be filled.

The initial consolations start to fade and this is perhaps why many give up the practice of silent prayer. In reality the journey is only just beginning and it is revealed as a journey into paradox. We often think of our spiritual lives as an attempt to get close to God, but in fact we are already deeply united with him. As we saw in previous chapters, the spiritual journey doesn't require intelligence or cleverness. Even the simplest of us can find our way into real union with God by a simple act of love. Every human being is qualified to make this journey but, as Jesus describes in the parable of the sower, not everyone responds in the same way. The paradox is that we do not initiate this journey; it is always a response to the prompting of the Spirit within.

The journey, however, demands effort and persistence on our part. The danger is that spirituality has become fashionable in some quarters today, even trendy, but this is no picnic and it will radically undermine our desire for control. Silent prayer is so counter-intuitive to our modern world. We have been brought up to think that we could increasingly control our environment. We thought we could live in a predictable universe in which we knew what we wanted to achieve and get from life. All we had to do was set out our goals and *go for it*. With our rational minds and a good education we have been led to believe that everything makes sense, that we can understand things. Life was no longer a mystery but a set of problems that our minds could solve. We were the ultimate problem solvers; we no longer needed the religious myth of salvation, because in the words of the Beatles song, *We can work it out.*

This mentality is typical of the mindset of most people today: it is the rational scientific mindset. It is essentially dualistic. This has consequences not just for our personal lives but also for how we relate to other nations, religions and cultures. Healthy religion starts with dualistic thinking then moves beyond it to reach the non-dual mystery. This is the critical gift that religion can give to our world today, to help us move beyond the conflicts that create so much violence and divisions to a vision that embraces a unified humanity. This unity has to include, not exclude, diversity and differences. Is this the face that religion presents to the world today? Sadly the great religions of the world often appear to be trapped in dualistic conflicts: Christian and Muslim, Muslim and Jew. What should be a reconciling and peaceful force has been turned into an antagonistic one.

The good news is that a growing number of people are seeking to go beyond the present stage of evolution thinking to embrace a new consciousness that can move beyond the rational need to explain and control everything and to break through to a higher level of consciousness. It is a consciousness that has always been present in the great religious founders and visionaries. Unfortunately their followers, with notable exceptions, were not always able to grasp it. Jesus warned his followers, specifically, not to put the new wine of this consciousness into old wineskins.

This new wine is called non-dual consciousness and it has been present in all the great religious founders. The Hindu Upanishads had this wisdom as did the Buddha, five or six centuries before Christ. Jesus has been described as the first non-dual teacher of the West and his teaching about the kingdom of God is not about a new kind of power structure—unless we call it a powerless structure—but a new kind of consciousness, a new way of seeing and a new way of being. This vision of realised oneness, expressed by the great religious founders, was understood and lived by the saints and the mystics. It is interesting to note that few mystics have been canonised. In a way this is not surprising. The saints lived the realised oneness that Jesus taught in his two great one-liners: *The Father and I are One,* and *Whatever you do to the least of these brothers and sisters of mine you do to me.* That kind of life lived in an exemplary way speaks to everyone, and so we seek to beatify and canonise people like Francis of Assisi, Francis of Sales, Don Bosco, Vincent de Paul, and many others. The mystics, on the other hand, tried to put these experiences of non-dual living into words. This is when theologians and Church authorities start to get a bit nervous because the mystics are trying to express a different kind of consciousness, one that could not be put into words.

Meister Eckhart is a classic case in point; he was condemned by the Church as a heretic. Today he has been rehabilitated. We need look no further than the conflicts between Jesus and the official religious leaders of his time. Sympathetic Pharisees like Nicodemus found Jesus hard to understand. When he revealed his teaching on the Eucharist many of his disciples left him, describing it as intolerable language. His apostles, including Peter, could not grasp his warnings about his suffering and death. Even after his resurrection some of the twelve are asking him, *Has the time now come to restore the kingdom to Israel.* What Jesus does is promise them that, as his physical presence is withdrawn from them, he will give them the gift of the Spirit who will lead them to a new level of understanding—*I still have many things to say to you, but you cannot bear them now. When the Spirit of truth comes, he will guide you into all the truth.*[28]

---

28 John 16:12-13

This is why Jesus begins his ministry with the summons to change our way of thinking and seeing (metanoia). We often speak in religious circles about the need for conversion, and the mystics also speak about conversion. In recent years spiritual teachers have spoken increasingly about different levels of consciousness, different ways of seeing.[29] This is really what conversion is about. When I was a student of philosophy I was introduced to the work of the Canadian Jesuit, Bernard Lonergan. He recognised that the scientific mind had destroyed any remnants of thinking of God as a kindly old man in the sky. He knew that theology had to face up to the challenges of the secular enlightenment. While he acknowledged that challenge, he also maintained that religion had a lot to offer in the search for truth, especially with regard to how we see.

Bernard Lonergan felt that religious believers tend to overdo their truth claims, especially with regard to understanding truth. He contrasted the apparent certitudes of religious believers with the willingness of scientists to create tentative theories and to test them out. Lonergan doesn't deny the objectivity of truth but he taught the need to clarify our subjectivity. He called this process *conversion*. For Lonergan a crucial part of this process is an awareness of how our egos can get in the way of the search for truth. I know this is true in my own life when I am more concerned to score points rather than seek a real experience of mutuality. I see it often with politicians who seek to defeat an opponent, even humiliate them, rather than create a shared search for truth. Authentic conversion means living from a different centre, that deeper appreciation of the shared gift of being that is the touchstone of our humanity. It involves a kind of cleansing of the lens of the seer, the observer. Such clear-seeing leads to an ability to distinguish what is essential, from what is secondary. This leads to the mystical insight that being is essentially, *Being-in-Love*. We don't so much grasp the truth as find ourselves being grasped by the truth. What Lonergan, and others such as Martin Buber (who said that all real living was *meeting*), seem to be saying is that truth demands some level of personal transformation, which is built on the mystical insight

---

29 See Michael Cunningham *Let Your Heart Pray*, Chapter 5(Don Bosco Publications 2009)

that everything is one. Truth is relational. We might disagree at the level of ideas but we recognise our fundamental common humanity.

From a Christian and mystical perspective, it all points to entering into the consciousness of Christ which is the stream of love that flows between Father and Son and is made available to us in the gift of the Spirit. Ultimate reality is revealed not by God's splendid isolation in the heavens, but is inherently relational. It is a communion of love. The purpose of our lives is not to construct for ourselves an isolated castle to protect ourselves against others, but to surrender that very desire for control and fall into the abyss of a mystery that calls us to relationship, to intimacy, to shared communion.

Without this kind of empathy we slip back into a more divisive consciousness. Instead of recognising our own limitations we seek to push our *certainties* on to others. Too many religious believers turn into anti-gays, anti-immigrants, anti-foreigners, anti-women, anti-Muslims, while claiming to be followers of Jesus. The mystics teach us that if we are to heal the world's pain we have to make the inner journey where our pain is opened up to the healing presence of the Spirit. This process is called prayer, not so much saying prayers in which the ego can remain in control, but a willingness to empty ourselves of our egos and learn the mystery of real presence. It is a way of unknowing, a way of paradox, that can deal with the ambiguities of life's mystery.

Chapter 7 — Beyond the Fear of God

Spiritual transformation is often thought of as movement from darkness to light. In one sense that is true, but in another sense it is totally false. We forget that darkness is always present alongside the light. Pure light blinds, only the mixture of darkness and light allows us to see. Shadows are required for our seeing. God alone lives in perfect light.[30]

In this chapter I want to move more deeply into the question of why dealing with the paradoxes of life is so important in the spiritual journey. We see so many contradictions around us in relations between nations, in politics, in religions, within families, and most of all, within our own lives. The dualistic mind is quick to see contradictions and moves quickly to easy judgements as to who is right and who is wrong, who is in and who is out, who is worthy and who is unworthy. In contrast, the more contemplative mind, what we are calling the non-dual mind, is able to deal with paradox and contradictions much more creatively. In a way it's surprising that Christians struggle with contradictions, and have become so riddled with divisions. Think of the enormous variety of Christian denominations in the world. How is it that we have got so caught up in splits and separations?

When the mystics speak about their experience of God they immediately adopt the language of paradox and reveal that the spiritual journey is the place where we have to learn to hold and not dismiss the tension of opposites. For example when they speak about the mystery of God they use words like *abyss* and *ground*. For the dualistic mind these are contradictory, but the mystics move to a different place, a different mind. The contemplative or non-dual mind creates space in which contradictory words can be held in creative tension; then a deeper truth emerges: both of these words are

---

30 Richard Rohr *Hope against Darkness* (St Anthony Messenger Press 2001) p164

experienced as carrying some truth. The more we can surrender ourselves to the abyss of God's love the more we discover the solidity of the ground on which we stand. A word like *abyss* might suggest a rather scary void, but the mystics assure us that this void is at the same time a holding void, a secure void, a foundational void. What this means is that I no longer have to ask whether I am doing it right or wrong, or about my level of worthiness, because I am being held. As Richard Rohr often says, the word *mystery* is not something totally beyond our knowledge; it is, in fact, endless *knowability*. This is exactly what the mystics confirm as they struggle to use words and metaphors to describe this depth experience. They point the way to unconditional love, endless care, infinite compassion, but unless we can experience this it is hard to believe it.

John of the Cross says that any experience of God has to be an experience of the unfamiliar. So if your piety and practice only keep you within your comfort zone of familiarity, where you can remain in control, you will not really know God. You might be able to speak and talk about God; but it will always be second-hand. This is why Jesus speaks so often about faith, not as an intellectual exercise, but as surrender to a mystery that both invites us to intimacy and yet is always beyond us.

The mystical journey is full of what has been called *the coincidence of opposites*, and it shouldn't surprise us when we recall how God leads us deeply into paradox in the central mystery of our faith: the death and resurrection of Jesus. In the spirituality of the first half of life we tend to build our spiritual identity on knowing what is right from what is wrong, knowing who is worthy and who is unworthy. In fact, the mystery of the Cross undoes that kind of thinking, the making of clear distinctions between good and evil. On the cross we see the great pattern of all spirituality revealed. The very worst event in human history, the killing of Jesus, turns into the very best, our salvation. This has to shatter our intellectual schemes to keep good and evil separate, because God takes the absolute worst event in history and turns it into the best. Our logical minds will always resist this. We like to keep clear blue water between good and evil, and position ourselves on the side of the good. The ego loves to do just that. I think all religions try to construct a moral framework of separation between good and evil, and Jesus spent much of his time challenging the purity codes of Jewish law and practice.

In fact the word *religion* should take us to a different place. It comes from the Latin word *re-ligio* and it means to bind together. Mature religion teaches us that no real transformation will happen unless we face our own shadow. We are used to modern psychology teaching us to deal with our problems, to try to overcome them. Carl Jung, however, knew that most of the problems we face in the second half of life are, in fact, spiritual. There will always be some problems that we cannot overcome and mature spirituality invites us to own them, to embrace them and even weep over them. I think this is what Jesus is trying to teach us when he says that those who mourn are blessed.

This is ancient spiritual wisdom that the dualistic mind cannot really grasp. The challenge of the second half of life is to learn to live with this tension of opposites—that we are, despite all our best efforts, always going to be a mixture of saint and sinner. This is a big defeat for the ego. On retreats I often tell of my experience as a Salesian novice. In those days we were being fed on the spirituality of perfection. I really bought into that in a big way and I set out to impress the novice master that I was the holiest novice and I would do this by being the first in the chapel every morning for prayer. So when the bell rang I shot out of bed, had a quick wash and rushed down into the chapel. Sadly for my proposed canonisation plan, there was always one other novice who got there before me. It was the same person every day. I would then spend my prayer time trying to think of ways of getting ahead of him. Maybe I could tie his shoelaces together, or trip him up a little as he went down stairs, anything to slow him down. Talk about an ego game! I was very unhappy with my failure. Perhaps, in my defence, I could point out that the prayer we were taught in those days was discursive meditation, not the prayer of silence. Discursive meditation is clearly a good way to pray but it can also keep the ego firmly in place.

After years of trying to own my shadow, I now realise that my shadow is, in fact, *failure*. A key step in this process for me was *the enneagram*[31] which taught me that I am a *six*, which means that while my virtue is loyalty, my sin is fear. The wisdom of the enneagram is that it reveals that all of us have a key strength and a key weakness. It is not a psychological game but a real tool for insight and discernment. It allows us to step back and see the contradictions of the human condition, that we are both saint and sinner. Both are part of who we are and both have to be acknowledged. I've also learned that many priests and religious have this personality type, the rather fearful but loyal person. I know this isn't the only reason but I think it is a significant factor in a lot of Christian formation, teaching in seminaries and schools, and preaching. Priests study theology before ordination but if there is no real spiritual direction or discernment or deep personal prayer then we will all pass on our fears to other people. If we have an unconscious, fearful image of God, that is what we will pass on to others. The enneagram teaches us to bring it to consciousness.

Past emphasis in Christian teaching has stressed the doctrinal truths of the faith. They are important and useful but they don't get us into the struggle that is at the heart of the spiritual journey. The Church has also invested a lot of time and personnel into education. Western education is very dualistic and in that sense has been very successful—consider all the achievements of our science and technology. Recent studies in spirituality are concentrating on the development of consciousness, and it is clear that lower levels are always dualistic. We learn our facts and information and the ego loves to use these so that we can win the argument with those who think differently than ourselves. You can ascend very high in the world of education, even get a Ph D, and yet be stuck at this lower level of dualistic consciousness.[32] The higher levels learn how to integrate the lower levels and move to a more non-dual way of thinking. Education is an important first step to the transformation of consciousness, but even the Church has tended to keep us at the lower levels of information, facts, and answers.

31 A system of analysis of possible personality types.
32 Michael Cunningham *Let Your heart Pray* (Don Bosco Publications 2009) see chapter 5

Not many formation programmes speak about transformation. The higher levels of consciousness lead naturally into mystery, into knowing and not-knowing at the same time. Non-dual thinking is a different way of seeing. It is not *either/or* thinking that seeks always to exclude, but is *both/and* thinking that sees the underlying unity of all things. This doesn't mean relativism, or subjectivism, but it does mean that we look for the ten, twenty, or fifty per cent of the truth that my enemy has. Above all else it recognises the *relational* dimension of truth.

Let me try to illustrate this by looking at the question of fear. Most Christians seem to have been brought up to fear God rather than to love him, as I pointed out in the first chapter. We may have been taught that if we do not behave properly, if we commit sins, God will punish us, and if the sin is really serious, God will torture us for all eternity. If that is true then it means that most human beings are far more loving and forgiving than God. Would you really want to torture someone for ever, for all eternity? No wonder we have created so many angry atheists.

Last summer, when on holiday, I attended a Sunday Mass in a parish in the United States. The celebrant was a young priest who gave the appearance of being very conservative. He wore his black cassock, he said parts of the Mass in Latin. I have to say he celebrated the liturgy with impressive reverence. In his homily he asked the question *Is God a loving god or is he a punishing god?* His answer was that, if we do not really behave well, God has to punish us. I have to say I got quite depressed as I listened to this undoubtedly well-intentioned young man. I could not help wondering about his prayer experience. What kind of God had he met in his heart? I hope I am not being too judgemental about him as I recalled my own ego-based prayer-life. Fortunately the Church is recovering a richer tradition of prayer and wisdom but I still suspect few formation programmes for priests and religious, and few catechetical programmes, are teaching the tradition of a more contemplative way of praying.

This fear-based image of God is very damaging to the spiritual journey, but it is deep seated in many people's lives. As the Benedictine Ian Petit points out:

> An emphasis on punishment can make God appear rather terrifying, and this has, I believe, blinded many people to the amazing truth of his mercy. Once you have seen God as someone to fear and dread, an immense amount of preaching on his mercy is needed to penetrate that wall of fear.[33]

In preaching retreats, in many parts of the world, I have come across this problem in the lives of a lot of priests, religious and laity: they want to love God, yet there is a lingering fear of unworthiness, and the teaching of a vengeful God reinforces that. If we impose our *either/or* mentality on God then it makes the central message of Jesus difficult to accept. At the same time, our dualistic thinking means that we don't know how to deal with the contradictions and mixed motives in our own lives. What happens is that we tend to deny and repress that side of ourselves. When that happens we then look around for someone else to carry our unresolved pain. The whole purpose of the spiritual journey is then lost and we stay at the lower levels of the first half of life—my individual struggle to become perfect, which is always, of course, doomed to failure. Many people today are walking away from this. In the Church we are presenting a God of love who is at the same time just waiting to punish us, even eternally, for our mistakes.

Mature religion should encourage us to face reality. Reality for all of us is mixed: the human condition is always a mixture of light and dark. This is the wisdom that the enneagram teaches: we all have our gift and we all have our wound, and this is shown in a rich variety of ways. It teaches us tolerance and compassion, and a sense of humour about our weaknesses. If we can't laugh at ourselves, we are in trouble spiritually. Rather than be ashamed of the complexity of the human condition, we need to be taught how to integrate it and give back

---

33 Ian Petit *God is not Angry* (Darton, Longman and Todd 1997) p37

to God the whole of what we are. We have tried to promote perfection at the cost of wholeness. It is in the paradoxes and contradictions of life that we meet God, not a punishing God, but the forgiving, inclusive and compassionate God of Jesus; who tells us he has come for us sinners not the so-called virtuous ones. Jesus didn't teach an ethic of perfection, but an ethic of consciousness. Such an ethic demands that we learn to own and not deny our shadow side.

The ego cannot win this battle. It has to learn to give up control and surrender to the abyss. Because of our past emphasis on correct answers and certitude we have distorted what Jesus means by faith. Faith for Jesus is trust in the relational truth of God's love for us, and the opposite of faith is not doubt, but fear and anxiety. A fearful image of God reduces religion to correct performance and behaviour. We still have priests today who want to turn away those who seek baptism for children if their parents are not attending church on a regular basis. We refuse Communion to those whose marriages have failed. We forget that, for Jesus, religion is not about purity codes, whereby the worthy are separated from the unworthy. Whenever Jesus meets purity codes he avoids them, challenges them, or ignores them.

If we are to discover a God of compassion and mercy, a God to whom we can surrender without fear there seem to be two authentic paths— prayer and suffering. Suffering occurs whenever we lose control. It is something we cannot fix. The choice then becomes stark: either fall into self-pity or reach a new level of relationship with a God who sustains and holds us. He may not take the pain away, but he carries it with us at a transformative level. Many saints and mystics experienced real suffering and yet lived their lives at a level of deep joy. I think this is true of many ordinary people, maybe not always educated in an intellectual sense, who fall into the abyss and find solid ground. We are fortunate to know such people.

The other path is, of course, prayer. In silent contemplative prayer we are led into the humiliation of the ego as we taste rather than deny our shadow selves. As we learn to observe our everyday thoughts and emotions it can be a very humiliating experience. As a lady said to me recently, *I had just spent time in adoration before the Blessed Sacrament, and then I went home and got so angry with somebody.* We can all identify with that, in some form or other. But the God of Jesus seems to want to meet and welcome all that we are, with our individual mixtures of light and dark. Here is where the transformation starts to happen, but it is not our work and achievement. All we have to learn is how to be present, fully present to God in all our contradictions. Then we learn to see what is real and accept it as *the naked now.* Contemplative prayer teaches us how to be present to this particular moment which is never going to be perfect. It is what it is, as the mystics teach us. The hardest thing we have to give to God is all that we are.

When married couples get beyond the early romanticism of their relationship, they begin to meet themselves and their partners in all their contradictions and frailties. This is when love really takes off, when they can say to each other, *I accept and love you as you are, warts and all.* Sexual intercourse then becomes what we call biblical knowing. The saints and mystics are those who have experienced this union of biblical knowing. They are at home with a God who has created us for infinite acceptance, infinite compassion, and infinite love.

Chapter 8 — The Divine Mystery: Beyond yet Intimate

I believe that God is drawing forth a new movement suitable for today's Christian contemplative life and practice. This can provide a Christian spiritual foundation for the globalizing world, just as the desert contemplative life did for the newly Christianized Roman world and as monastic life did later for the medieval European world.[34]

In his classic spiritual book, *The Idea of the Holy,* Rudolph Otto describes the encounter with God as an experience of paradox. He uses the phrases *mysterium tremendum* and *mysterium fascinosum,* the *tremendous mystery* and the *fascinating mystery.* An experience of the holy, for Otto, places us in the centre of these apparent contradictions. In this chapter I want to try to reflect on these apparent opposites, recognising that any attempt to describe God will always fail as our finite minds encounter the infinite mystery of God. But if we can hold the tension of the apparent contradictions we can move into the authentic mystery that is at the same time both beyond and yet intimately surrounding us.

The *mysterium tremendum* emphasises the awesomeness of God. It is the *Holy, Holy, Holy* that we sing with the angels. It is the beyond, the beyond of a transcendent mystery. It is God far and above us. In many ways this is the image of God of the first half of life. It reinforces my sense of radical unworthiness and sinfulness. It is Simon Peter, having witnessed the miraculous catch of fish, falling to his knees before Jesus with the words, *Go away from me, Lord, for I am a sinful man!*[35] Peter discovers that, far from recoiling from his unworthiness, Jesus is calling him to an intimate and close friendship. So the *mysterium tremendum* needs to be balanced by the *mysterium fascinosum.* While the

---

34 David Frenette, *Spirituality, Contemplation & Transformation, Chapter 2 Three Contemplative Waves* (Lantern Books, NY 2008) p11
35 Luke 5:8

mysterium tremendum stresses the otherness and the greatness of God the *mysterium fascinosum* reveals the attraction, the allurement, the enticement at the heart of this mystery. There is a sense that I am being pulled into something that has endless fascination. It is a seduction, a delight, a love affair.

An experience of the holy is therefore an entering into the mystery of paradox. One of the earliest writers to use this language of the coincidence of opposites was Nicholas of Cusa, a fifteenth century ambassador to the Vatican. He taught that God was both incomprehensible and always beyond our minds, and at the same time inviting us into a relationship of great intimacy. Like the author of the *The Cloud of Unknowing* and so many other mystics, he taught that we have to learn to accept that we don't know. In any encounter with God we have to leave our rational minds behind and enter the darkness with love. Once again, it is a movement from control to surrender. We then discover that this transcendent mystery has secretly chosen each one of us. It is very personal. This is bridal mysticism, and it reflects Jesus' use of the banquet feast as the image of life in the kingdom. The people who thought themselves unworthy of God—sinners, tax collectors, prostitutes—are the very ones who receive the invitation.

I am not sure that the Church has always led us into this intimate relationship with God. As the mystical tradition was side-lined for centuries, we have tended to reduce the spiritual life to an individual struggle with our sinfulness. We can never be worthy of the *mysterium tremendum*—and this, of course, is true—but we neglected the other half of the mystery: the tenderness, the mercy, the compassion and the forgiveness of God. We taught from dualistic minds, identifying divisions between the worthy and the unworthy, the good and the bad. You can see this clearly in the very sacrament of union and communion that Jesus gave us, the Eucharist. Instead of the inclusiveness of Jesus who frequently eats with sinners we have turned it into a worthiness contest, and have created an exclusion zone around it. Having said that, we also need to recognise that the *mysterium tremendum* demands that we approach it with reverence and respect. You don't accept an invitation to a wedding feast and proceed to disrespect the bride and groom. Both aspects of the mystery need to be honoured and recognised.

Because we have not been taught to trust the call to intimacy in prayer, we tend to be suspicious of the idea and this is exacerbated by our Catholic tradition with its emphasis on clear doctrinal teaching, the search for certainty mentioned in earlier chapters. In recent years there has been a lot of work done in terms of stages of development. James Fowler looked at stages of faith development, Lawrence Kohlberg studied stages of moral development, and more recently others such as Ken Wilbur and Richard Rohr are looking at different levels of consciousness.[36] Some say there are nine levels, some eight or seven, but the key point is that the lower levels of consciousness are very dualistic and the higher levels move into non-dual, or unitive seeing. The invitation to love that the mystics describe is essentially non-dual. It is what spiritual teachers call *beginner's mind*, or *the contemplative mind* and it can only be accessed through love. The term is used because the mystery of God is infinitely beyond, so we are always beginners. For the mystics, our lives are about transformation into Love, a participation in the very life of God who is Being-in-Love. Far from shying away from mystery, contemporary theologians, such as Bernard Lonergan, Karl Rahner and William Johnston invite us into the experience of falling in love with God.

These theologians remind us that we have all been created to experience directly the love of God in our hearts. We may never reach the seventh heaven of Teresa of Avila or St Paul, but the invitation and call to mysticism is open to all human beings. In chapter two I spoke of my experience of baptising baby Damien and encountering the loving heart of a child who lived a mere three weeks. The whole human family has been created by God to share in his own Being-in-Love. In this sense spirituality is revealed not as an optional extra, but the very core and goal of our life. Despite the fragmentation, confrontation and violence in much of our world today a new consciousness of this call to union and unity is emerging across the globe. We have become familiar

---

36 See chapter 5 of *Let your Heart Pray.*

with the word *globalisation* and tend to see it in an economic sense; but in its fullest sense what is happening today is *spiritual globalisation*.

While this spiritual awakening is a personal one, in that we are all secretly chosen to be intimate with God, the more we descend into the deepest centre of our souls the more we touch the source of all Being that is God. Our sense of being chosen is shared by everybody and this opens us to the paradox that our personal spiritual journey unites us with every other being. The journey within becomes the journey without. The source of our being comes from beyond us; we do not initiate the journey of love and union. We have to learn to detach ourselves from our ordinary psychological awareness of everyday thoughts and feelings because they cannot, of themselves, hold and carry the mystery. Our egos are not big enough to carry this mystery; they are desperate to hold on to the agenda of the false self; *am I being successful, does this make me look good?* This prevents us from truly letting go, which is the heart of all authentic spirituality and falling into the eternal Being, from which everything arises.

The mystics are those who have made the journey into their deepest selves before us and they have directly experienced the God who is at the same time both beyond and yet intimate. The call to intimate union can happen at any time in our lives. The author of *The Cloud of Unknowing* says that there comes a moment in our lives when it is almost impossible to ignore God's persistent knocking at the door of our soul. John of the Cross speaks about the wound of love. For St Augustine, God is closer to us than we are to ourselves. But this is not an easy path and we have to be prepared to meet the resistances that have to be broken down, as our false self fights to stay in control. Jesus puts it very bluntly in terms of a struggle between control and surrender:

> Those who want to save their life will lose it, and those who lose their life will save it.[37]

---

37 Matthew 16:25

As busy people, we tend to interpret the task of losing our life in terms of self-sacrifice and the giving of ourselves generously in activity and in service of others. Of course this is a vital part of our living of the gospel; it must flow into self-sacrificing love and compassionate service, especially for those less fortunate than ourselves. My own religious congregation, the Salesians of Don Bosco, has a long and proud tradition of service to the young and the poor. I have been privileged to see wonderful works in different parts of the world. There can be a danger, however, that the ego can thrive in such activity, especially if we neglect the inner journey. It is perfectly possible to work hard for God without an intimate relationship. We like to keep God at a distance.

I was struck recently by some remarks made by Fr Pascual Chavez, the Rector Major of the Salesians. Speaking on the 150th anniversary of the founding of the Salesian Congregation,[38] he described our Salesian heresy as *activism*. He said that while we have studied in great detail the history of our founder Don Bosco, and his pedagogical methods, we have not made ourselves sufficiently aware of his spirituality, and he called on us to become *contemplatives-in-action*. It is not that activity is bad but it is more a case of who is doing it with us. Is our activity coming from ourselves or from a deeper and more abundant source? It is a question of learning how to align ourselves with the source of all love that is God. This God is not out there waiting to judge us for our failures, but is present in the depths of our being where he holds us in a constant loving embrace. For us to become more aware of the holy mystery that we are, involves some letting go of our limited self-image and the attempt to live more consciously the truth of who we are in God. This is the transformation Paul describes when he says *it is no longer I who live but it is Christ who lives in me.*[39] It demonstrates that our value and worth is not just psychological, it is rooted in an ontological, metaphysical foundation which nothing can shake.

38 *Acts of the General Council of the Salesian Congregation May-August 2010* n407
39 Galatians 2:20

When we are really centred in our true identity we discover a different way of being and a different way of seeing. Instead of trying to shape other people the way we like them to be, we learn to be more open and receptive. We all share the same deep capacity for God and the purpose of life is to let it unfold and flow through us. We discover that God doesn't take sides and that he is immensely patient with our inability to live fully compassionate lives. We find an incarnational way of seeing everything as arising out of Being-in-Love. Gradually we Christians are learning that the whole universe is one evolutionary flow and we human beings are the conscious part of that universe. That, in itself, ought to give us a foundational humility with regard to what we know and what we don't know about this unfolding mystery. We discover that God is present in everything and everyone: the *mysterium tremendum* is revealed in a flower, a plant, a star, the face of a child, or an elderly person, and above all, in the human heart. Here is where the *mysterium fascinosum* attracts our poets, our dramatists, our artists and, especially today, our scientists. We learn to see other religions not as rivals but as fellow searchers for the truth; even the anger of militant atheism and secularism has something to teach us. Their anger with religion is not unconnected with our rather small tribal images in which we have tried to domesticate the wildness of the mystery.

The journey into holiness is not the search for moral perfection but the realisation that we are all participants in an unfolding mystery that we cannot control. All we have to do is to stay in union, to stay connected. Our recent Western history of spiritual individualism has led us down the narrow path of a moral struggle to *save our souls*. Instead we find ourselves, with all humanity, inside the mystery of radical grace. God, in Jesus, chose to hide himself inside the material world. There is no longer any division between sacred and secular, as we saw in chapter four. The mystery of radical grace breaks all rules and we see the official religious leaders of the time thrown into a panic by the grace of forgiveness that Jesus is freely offering to all and sundry. There is no evil in anything created by God, nor can anything of his block our union with him. The only obstacle in the way is our false self, that is our deep need to hang on to our separate egoic sense of who we are. Why do we do this? Eckhart Tolle provides an insightful answer:

> Why does the ego play roles? Because of one unexamined assumption, one fundamental error, one unconscious thought. That thought is: *I am not enough.* Other unconscious thoughts follow: *I need to play a role in order to get more so that I can be more.* But you cannot be more than you are because underneath your physical and psychological form, you are one with Life itself, one with Being. In form you will always be inferior to some, superior to others. In essence, you are neither inferior nor superior to anyone. True self-esteem and true humility arise out of that realization. In the eyes of the ego, self-esteem and humility are contradictory. In truth they are one and the same.[40]

The overcoming of the dualistic split between self-esteem and humility leads us to the peace and joy which the world of dualism cannot understand. No matter what is happening on the surface of their lives the mystics testify to this foundational experience of the gifts of the Spirit. It can be ours too. We can never be free of our ego and we need to allow it to function properly, by letting the true, authentic self to emerge. We do this when we allow the light of consciousness to shine on our ego. We move from cleverness to wisdom. It is a move from our limited thoughts and emotions to seeing with the eye of the heart. Spiritual teachers call this *Big Heart*. Jesus called it *a Second Birth*. It is not about becoming a shiny new version of who we think we are; that is going to die anyway. What dies are our illusions of what we think is real. We then begin to see reality as it is, not as we try to fit it into our limited dualistic perspective. This is kingdom consciousness; it belongs to the pure of heart and the poor and humble in spirit.

---

40 Eckhart Tolle *A New Earth* (Penguin Books London 2005) p109

Chapter 9 — The Inner Witness

One of the great paradoxes of the spiritual life is that our struggles are not separate from the luminous vastness within each of us. We don't get rid of struggle to discover this open space; nor does its discovery necessarily rid us of our struggles. The riddle of the obstacle is solved not by pushing it away or by holding on to it, but by meeting it with silence and by discovering in this meeting that sacred ground, which upholds both joy and sorrow, both struggle and freedom from struggle.[41]

Contemplative spirituality has been described as a long loving look at what is real. It sees and recognises the underlying unity in everything that exists. This unitive vision is foundational wisdom and is brilliantly described in The Garden of Eden as *The Tree of Life*. All that exists is good: God saw all that he made and found it very good. Adam and Eve, however, chose to eat the fruit of another tree, the tree of knowledge of good and evil. This gave us knowledge rather than wisdom, because it broke the underlying unity of all things and led us into dualistic judgements such as right and wrong, good and bad, male and female, superior and inferior, subject and object, me and you. Locked into the *me world* we became self-centred. We lost the unitive way of seeing, enjoyed in *The Garden*, and were thrown into a world where we need boundaries to secure our identity with family and tribe. We became defensive and fearful of *the other.* Boundaries are necessary as we grow into maturity, but because of our egocentric vision, our dualistic judgements keep us inside them. So *my tribe is better than your tribe, my country is better than your country, my religion is better than your religion.* Here lie the seeds of so much division, war and conflict throughout human history. Our dualistic minds have produced incredibly destructive weaponry. We can now destroy all life on the planet. But our consciousness has not grown sufficiently with these developments and political leaders are still

---

41 Martin Laird *Into The Silent Land* (Darton, Longman & Todd London 2008) p115

prepared to go down the path of violence and destruction as a means of solving human differences. Hence the crisis of our times. Any rejection of the other shares in that violence.

The good news for our times is the emergence of an evolutionary story of creation that includes all our stories and reveals the growth in complexity and consciousness at the heart of all creation. In theological terms we discover that God is continually communicating himself to us in love. Traditionally, religions have set great store by God's communication through sacred scripture and the teaching authority of the Church, but now we are more aware that God has been at the heart of the unfolding creation story that began 13.7 billion years ago. We are learning so much from scientists, and discovering even more that we cannot know. We are learning to welcome mystery.

> One way to speak of the Christian story is to say that God is always doing something more. Incomprehensible holy mystery is always giving more, revealing more, communicating more. The only limit to that giving has been creation's capacity to receive. A look back over the history of creation suggests that as our species has continued to evolve, our capacity to recognise and respond to the holy has grown.[42]

Our increasing ability to respond creatively to the presence of the infinite mystery is central to the work of those who are studying the development of consciousness. Centuries back, humanity saw God as above and beyond, the *mysterium tremendum* that we spoke of in the last chapter. Thunder, lightning, natural disasters all had to be appeased by sacrificial offerings. As evolution unfolded, humanity developed the capacity to reflect and become aware of the presence of the sacred in special places and, increasingly, in humanity itself. For Christians, Jesus is the man with total receptivity to God, whom he addresses in intimate language, as *Abba, Father*. There is no ego agenda in Jesus: all he wants to do is the will of the Father:

---

42 Judy Cannato *Field of Compassion* (Sorin Books, Notre Dame, Indiana 2010) p98

I tell you the Son can do nothing on his own but only what he sees the Father doing....I can do nothing on my own. As I hear I judge; and my judgement is just, because I seek to do not my own will but the will of Him who sent me.[43]

His mission is to proclaim the kingdom of God, which is not a place, but a new consciousness, a new kind of awareness of God's loving presence in the world. All are invited to share the new wine of this consciousness.

An evolutionary universe is a place of continuous becoming. Nothing is perfect. God's communication always holds something back. Our finite minds can never contain the infinite. Jesus is fully aware that people will respond differently to this new kind of consciousness, as he shows in the parable of the sower. Even his closest disciples will only have an inkling of what he is saying; much more will gradually be revealed, and this cannot happen while Jesus is still physically present to them:

I still have many things to say to you, but you cannot bear them now. When the Spirit of truth comes, he will guide you into all the truth; for he will not speak on his own, but will speak whatever he hears, and he will declare to you the things that are to come.[44]

The Spirit is our Inner Witness, the pure gift and presence of God within, the source of wisdom. In our time, the Spirit of God is awakening many people across the world to a more conscious way of living. For many centuries the Catholic Church has located this teaching of the Spirit in the papacy and the hierarchical structures, and these remain vital and important guides. Today there is an increasing recognition that the Spirit is given to the laity as well as bishops and priests. The Second Vatican Council was a real step forward as the term *People of God* became increasingly used. Sadly, in recent years there seems to have been some resistance to this idea as the hierarchical and curial structures have reasserted a more controlling model of authority.

---

43 John 5:19,30
44 John 16:12-13

But the Spirit continues to blow where She will and the emergence of a more contemplative style of praying and living is a clear sign of this.

Hopefully, the recovery of this more mystical way of knowing will grow in conjunction with the support of the hierarchical structure. What is clear is that we are discovering more practical ways of accessing the power of the Spirit within, and this teaching is encouraging a more mature spirituality to emerge, particularly in relation to the paradoxical nature of the spiritual journey. More and more people want to move beyond *the first half of life* agenda, with its boundaries, its laws and morality structure, its understanding of religion as a belonging structure. They are at home in *the second half agenda*: compassion, forgiveness, wisdom, knowing and not knowing, carrying the mystery of joy and sorrow.

Moving beyond doesn't mean jettisoning, because a crucial element of new levels of knowing is that they always integrate and build on former stages. It means moving beyond the rather black and white opinions of the first half of life to accepting the complexities of the second half of life. We cannot do this unless we learn how to deal with the imperfections and contradictions of our own journey and open ourselves to the spirituality of imperfection. The presence of the Spirit is the transforming agent in our souls.

Spiritual awareness, today, recognises the need to move beyond the ego-based rational consciousness with its dualisms, which has dominated Western culture, both secular and religious, in recent centuries, to a more unified way of seeing—a way of seeing that reflects reality, not just as I see it, but as it truly is. The key to this is learning how to connect with what spiritual guides call the *The Witness,* or as it is sometimes referred to as *The Inner Witness*, or *The Stable Witness*.

As long as we remain trapped in our ordinary everyday consciousness we stay victims of the endless stream of thought and emotions that exist in our chattering minds. In *The Power of Now* Eckhart Tolle describes the ego as *the unobserved mind*. It simply cannot separate itself from the endless chatter and reactive emotions that form the soap opera of our everyday lives and awareness. We become totally trapped in this way of looking at everything from our own limited point of view. To live more conscious lives we have to find a way of detaching ourselves from the psychodrama of the self-centred mind.

Most people tend to react to events and other people by analysing things over and over again in their minds. It can be useful sometimes to do this, but more often than not we get caught up in the same knee-jerk and repetitive reactions. You can see why the saints and mystics talked so much about detachment. The hardest thing to let go of is our own fixed reactions to people and situations that we meet. Spiritual teachers speak about the need to detach ourselves from surface events and find the place of the *Stable Witness*. Our separate egos cannot escape the pattern of seeing and judging everything and everybody from our own point of view. This is nothing to do with intelligence or education; you can have the highest educational qualifications and still be trapped in ego consciousness and be totally egocentric.

We have therefore to find an objective, calm, non-judging Observer, a place where we can stand and see ourselves playing our reactive games. This is a wisdom we have largely lost and it is rarely taught in the Churches, as we get locked into the moral improvement tasks of the first half of life, most of which take place under the gaze of a disapproving God: a God reduced to a driving-test examiner waiting to note and record our every mistake. One of the gifts of a more contemplative spirituality is to move to this inner space which observes our thoughts and emotions not with a critical gaze, but a deeply compassionate one

This is why so many spiritual teachers, including Jesus, say that spirituality is much more about seeing than doing. If we can learn to see rightly then our doing will be correctly aligned with who we really are, in God. We can escape the narrow vision of the ego which has to keep dividing the field with negative judgements. We move to the place of compassionate seeing, where everything belongs. As we learn to become detached observers of our own false selves we learn how to look at ourselves with compassion rather than judgement. This takes time because a lot of religious formation makes us analytical and judgemental. Instead of letting reality be what it is, we quickly move into categorising it as good or bad, moral or immoral. If you think this is being soft and liberal, look at how Jesus meets people in the gospel. When he meets the Samaritan woman, for example, he doesn't impose a moral agenda on her, but he places her life within a larger narrative and from that position of respect for her he summons her to a fuller life.

The practice of the Inner Witness is part of the recovery of our true identity as children of God. This larger context of who we are is able to look at our small self with understanding and compassion. It allows us to include the more fearful aspect of our small self, in the safe recognition that it doesn't define all of who we are. It helps us to live with the mystery that we are all a mixed blessing. Instead of being afraid of reality and wanting to fix it to be more like us, we can learn to embrace it and open ourselves to the paschal pattern of joy and sorrow, of light and dark, that is the Big Pattern, the Big Story, the Great love, the Great Mystery of infinite love in which everything arises. As Richard Rohr explains:

> Jesus tells us in the gospels, *Don't be afraid.* He's saying it is radically okay. You can trust yourself because God trusts you, using your journey, your experience. Nothing will be wasted; all has been forgiven; nothing will be used against you. In fact, God will even use your sins to transform you!...If that's not the *good news* what else could it be?[45]

Paul touches on the same theme in his letter to the Romans:

> The Spirit himself and our spirit **bear united witness** that we are children of God.[46]

---

45 Richard Rohr *Everything Belongs* (The Crossroad Publishing Company NY 2003) p129
46 Romans 8:16

This is a crucially important teaching in which Paul is pointing to the Inner Witness, which becomes a united witness when my spirit is joined to the Holy Spirit. This is the greatest difference between Christian contemplation and Eastern forms of meditation: the indwelling gift of the Spirit. Buddhism, for example has developed a very sophisticated language to describe the mind and the compulsive self, or false self. As the Western Church lost much of the contemplative tradition in recent centuries we forgot that we had this kind of teaching in our tradition, and it tends to be framed in language of a different age that we don't easily understand these days. Words like *passions* get interpreted by us to mean sex, which is not what these teachers were talking about. For them, passions refer to the pattern of compulsive-addictive behaviours that afflicts all of us. The primary form of addictive behaviour is the addiction to our own way of thinking, living in what Tolle calls the unobserved mind. A very practical way of becoming conscious of this is called *welcoming prayer.*

The Welcoming Prayer

We are told in the scriptures to *put on the mind of Christ*, and this is not just a case of trying to be kind and compassionate like Jesus, but of awakening to the centre of our being where the Spirit of Jesus, the Holy Spirit dwells. It is not just thinking in a new way, but of reaching a place of inner alignment, our heart's centre where God lives within. We often read about the divine indwelling; welcoming prayer, like Centering Prayer, is a way of accessing, or at least opening ourselves to this deepest centre. Here we find the *purity of heart* that Jesus promises will always see God. It provides access to a different field of energy from our ordinary consciousness.

Welcoming prayer has three stages. It takes the oppositional energy of the egoic mind and redirects it into your body, so that you can be freed from the power of the false self. It recaptures this energy at a more spiritual level. Instead of being pushed and pulled around by the oppositional energy, you learn to focus it at a deeper level. It takes it into your true being, your inner centre, your true self. We bring the unconscious and unfocused energy into a deeper awareness. So the first step is to *feel* whatever pain or anger you are experiencing. Instead of trying to deny it, just feel it. When we are attacked we tend to want to fight back. In this method you are asked not to do this but to actually feel the emotion and take it to the place of the Stable Witness. This is not easy to do but it can be developed with repeated practice.

The second stage is not to push away and reject the emotion, but to *welcome it*. Try saying *Welcome pain*, or, *Welcome anger*. Doing this has already created the Inner Observer because you have separated yourself from the emotion. Welcoming takes away some of its negative energy. You are learning to observe that the anger is not you, because you can look back at it. The anger is an emotion; it is not your whole being. You can escape the knee-jerk response of the false self to defend yourself, or go on the attack. So the second step is to welcome the difficult situation and the feelings that go with it. This is truly transforming.

Having felt the emotion, and welcomed it—and we should not rush this —we can be free to let it go. This letting go is the third and final stage of welcoming prayer. A suggested formula is:

> I let go my desire for security and approval.
> I let go my desire for esteem and affection.
> I let go my desire for power and control.
> I let go my desire to change the situation.

This is the spirituality of surrender mentioned in earlier chapters. The first three points address the false self energy centres. The fourth point allows us to embrace what is, and be present fully to it. It doesn't mean that we should not change unjust situations, but it means that my energy to change comes from a different place: not anger but compassion.

We tend to be taught to act on our emotions or deny them. Welcoming prayer feels the emotion so that you do not lose the gift of *presence, awareness of your true self, who you really are in God*. The difference therefore, between Christian and Eastern forms of meditation is that we don't have to create the Stable Witness; it is already there: it is the gift of the Spirit. All we have to do is to be awakened to it and our true self bears common witness, as Paul says, with the Spirit of God.

Baby Damien, in the mere three weeks of his life, taught me that we are all, without exception, created to receive love and to give love. Our small selves protect ourselves with fear-filled defences in which we hurt both ourselves and others. We have to take these hurts from our sad selves into our loved selves, our true self which is united in the *Body* of Christ with the *Spirit* of Christ; the place where we are always loved unconditionally, despite whatever we may have done. As with Jesus in Gethsemane, the pain may not go away but it loses its power to overcome the foundational joy and love that is the true self within. We learn to accept whatever the present moment offers us and we transform it with loving acceptance. The fourteenth century German Dominican, Johann Tauler used to say that God made our capacity for goodness the innermost part of us and it is closer to us than we are to ourselves. That is our life awakened in the Spirit.

Chapter 10—Active and Contemplative

The spiritual life is not a specialized part of daily life. Everything you do in the day, from washing to eating breakfast, having meetings, driving to work, solving problems, making more problems for yourself once you have solved them, watching television, or deciding instead to read, going to a restaurant, or going to a movie, or going to church, everything you do is your spiritual life. It is only a matter of how consciously you do these ordinary things, how attentive you are to the opportunities they offer for growth, for enjoyment, and how mindfully, selflessly, how compassionately you perform them. Yet to live life spiritually all the time everyone needs to take specific times to focus on the spiritual dimension before everything else.[47]

Thomas Aquinas was asked the question: which is the most important vocation in the Church, the active life or the contemplative life? He answered that the most important vocation was the integration of the two. I think this is one of the most important issues in contemporary spirituality. It addresses the problem of dualistic thinking as it infects even the spiritual journey. We can see this dualism even in the pattern of official religious life which, with a few exceptions, splits between active and contemplative styles. I'm not saying that the two forms should merge, but I am suggesting a better balance within existing congregations. The task of integration that Aquinas underlined was ignored, as the Church at almost all levels lost the contemplative tradition, especially around the time of the Reformation and the Enlightenment.[48] We moved from Jesus, teaching that the pure in heart will see God, to Descartes *I think therefore I am.* It was called the Enlightenment!

---

47 Bede Griffiths *The Mystery Beyond* (Medio Media/Arthur James London 1997) p8
48 See Cynthia Bourgeault *Centering Prayer and Inner Awakening* Ch6 The Loss and Recovery of the Christian Contemplative Tradition (Cowley Publications 2004)

As a result the active religious orders prayed solely in what was called the *kataphatic* tradition. This consisted of verbal prayer using words, music, and images; and even meditation became discursive prayer or *thinking* about God. The long tradition of silent, non-verbal, or *apophatic* prayer as it was called, which abandons all thought, concepts and ideas about God in favour of direct experience of God, fell by the wayside. This loss was so pervasive that even the contemplative orders themselves almost abandoned the *apophatic* way of praying. Prayer was reduced to saying prayers. While there were still individuals who lived a mystical life in these lean years, it was largely the work of Thomas Merton that brought the issue into the open in the middle of the last century. During the sixties many young people abandoned Christianity and turned to the East, to Hinduism and Buddhism for teaching in contemplative prayer. Merton got permission from his monastic superiors to travel to the East where he tragically met his death in 1968. Before he died he wrote to his monastic community and reminded them that everything he was learning about the Eastern tradition already existed in the West, but we had largely forgotten it. In the West the dualistic mindset ruled supreme.

The Protestant Reformation rightly critiqued some decadent aspects of Catholicism, but it stayed completely in the head. It was all about who had the right ideas about God. Trapped in the same dualistic mind the Catholics fought back with their ideas and concepts. Even though Protestants opened the scriptures to the laity with the aid of the vernacular and the newly-invented printing press it was still being read with a dualistic mind. Texts were not searched for wisdom but as tools for attacking opponents. As Richard Rohr observes, both sides argued about who had the right container and forgot to taste the wine. Compassion went out of the window, as we tortured and killed each other; all in the name of religion.

Contemplative spirituality teaches us how to see, accept and forgive reality. Instead of shaping it in the way I would like. I have to learn to receive it for what it is. This doesn't mean that action doesn't matter, but it has to come from a place of compassion. When we look at the life of Jesus, we tend to focus on what he did during his public ministry.

We think of those three years, although some scholars suggest it might have even been a shorter period. We forget that Jesus spent the first thirty or so years of his life in seclusion. His life pattern was more contemplative than active. Just when it appears that he is ready to begin his active ministry with his baptism in the Jordan, in fact he does the opposite—he goes into the desert for forty days and nights. When he eventually emerges to begin his work he is constantly described in the gospels as withdrawing from the crowds to spend time in prayer, as mentioned in chapter three. The baptismal moment for Jesus reveals the whole spiritual life as an experience of Sonship in relation to his Abba, Father, and he continually reminds people that he has come to do his Father's will not his own.

The question of the will of God is a very important one. While we have all been taught that we must do the will of God, it tends to be influenced by the first half of life agenda: we must obey God's laws, as they are imposed on us from on high. Disobedience leads to punishment, and since we all fail from time to time we are left wallowing in guilt for most of our lives. Many walk away—such a negative message cannot be good news. We forget that Jesus did not come to load heavy burdens of guilt on us—in fact he gets angry with the Pharisees and Scribes for doing just that—but to reveal to us the unconditional love of his Father. He wants to take away our fear-filled images of God and replace them with his own experience of intimacy and love. Because his Father allowed the sun to rise on good and bad men alike and the rain to fall on both just and unjust, Jesus is able to speak about God's compassion, love and forgiveness in a way that plainly shocked, not the sinners, but the religious teachers. They preferred a religion of observance and obedience to one of relationship and intimacy. It seems to me that without some kind of direct inner experience of God's unconditional love we don't really *get* Jesus or understand what he was doing. God's will isn't imposed from without; it is discovered within the heart.

I come back to the issues of control and surrender raised in the earlier chapters. The most difficult part of the spiritual journey is the giving-up of control of our lives, what I have called *surrendering to the mystery*.

We need to ask the question, does God want us to work for him or to love him? I can only offer a non-dual answer and say that it is both. We cannot just sit in contemplative prayer and ignore the pain and suffering of the world around us. One thing we can clearly say is that such prayer is not authentic Christian contemplation. On the other hand, if we just engage in action without some experience of intimacy the danger is that the ego will take control very quickly. So our action needs to be truly centred in the depths of our being, from a consciousness and awareness that we share in the gift of God's Being. We need both Martha and Mary. In our busy, extroverted culture today, whether religious or secular, we are more likely to find the balance tipped in favour of Martha. We are back to the Aquinas point: the need for the integration of the two. We need to act from a solid centre where God is in charge and pray in a way that both celebrates the wonderful beauty of creation, while remaining open to the pain of the world.

A contemplative living of the gospel knows that I don't have to do everything, and I don't have to know everything. All I need to do is to become an empty space so God's love and compassion can flow through me. This takes away a lot of anxiety. Many of the mystics speak about enlargement and rest as they meet God at ever-deepening levels. Living from our heart's true centre we are opened to the one gracious mystery of Being that arises and is continually granted to us. It brings a calmness and rest, a joy and peace that the world cannot give. It takes away that fixing mentality, that effort and striving which appears to be working for God, but is often masquerading as my ego. The Great Mystery, that we call the paschal mystery, teaches us that there is only One Sadness, the pain and crucifixion of Jesus, and only One Joy, the resurrection of Jesus. The contemplative gospel reveals that the private, separate ego will never understand this. The spiritual journey is always a matter of participation. Just stay connected to the vine, says Jesus. Tasting the pain in this way, welcoming it, as I suggested in the last chapter, means that it can never destroy you, but you can live with it. There is no need to keep striving to find the perfect place where all pain is eliminated.

With this kind of seeing we can begin to grasp why the saints gravitate towards the poor, because they are symbols of who we really are before God: naked and poor. Authentic contemplation takes us to the same place: naked and poor before God. This is the place where we encounter the unity of all things, and a God who excludes no one. As Desmond Tutu expresses it:

> In God's family there are no outsiders. All are insiders. Black and white, rich and poor, gay and straight, Jew and Arab, Palestinian and Israeli, Roman Catholic and Protestant, Serb and Albanian, Hutu and Tutsi, Muslim and Christian, Buddhist and Hindu, Pakistani and Indian—all belong.[49]

We discover the non-dual insight that we are God's Body. The only way to learn this is to see that the wounded person, the leper, the poor person, that I want to turn away from, is in fact a part of me. What we want to reject becomes the cornerstone. If we still don't want to believe this, Jesus himself becomes the ultimate victim. It's always the part of ourselves that we want to reject that is the place—*the narrow gate*—Jesus calls it, where we meet the compassion of God. We don't have to be perfect: we are called to be vulnerable, going beyond our comfort zones in welcoming the other, the stranger, the one who is different.

The Carmelite, William McNamara, describes contemplation as *a long loving look at the Real.* Some Christians just want to experience the suffering side of spirituality, others prefer the happier side. It needs to include both because God embraces everything and forgives everything. Perhaps the most difficult part of the spiritual life is to allow God to love us unconditionally, to know that we are *known through and through* and intimately embraced in all our preciousness and our brokenness. This kind of knowing cannot just be worked out in our minds, by human intelligence. It has to be felt at a cellular level. I know that men are not encouraged to weep openly in our Western

49 Desmond Tutu *God Has A Dream* (Rider, Random Publishing House, London 2005) p20

culture, but, as I get older, I find myself weeping more often in moments when the mystery draws nearer to me. My only response is to weep because words cannot express the depth of the mystery. I also find myself laughing more as I taste the joy of it all. Saint Ephrem taught that we only need two gifts in life: the gift of laughter and the gift of tears.

I am always struck by the point in the gospels when Jesus asks his disciples what people are saying about him:

> *Who do people say the Son of Man is?* And they said, *some say John the Baptist, but others Elijah, and still others Jeremiah or one of the prophets.* He said to them, *Who do you say I am?* Simon Peter answered, *You are the Messiah, the Son of the living God.* And Jesus answered him, *Blessed are you, Simon, son of Jonah! For flesh and blood has not revealed this to you, but my Father in heaven.*[50]

It is a very personal question, centred on their relationship to him. He doesn't really want to know what others are saying, he makes the question direct and personal: *Who do you say I am?* Jesus reveals to Peter that his answer hasn't come from human intelligence or cleverness. It is a special kind of *knowing* which Peter has experienced. Jesus is talking here about a contemplative, intuitive, inner kind of knowing. It reveals to Peter and the other disciples an experience of profound intimacy. Jesus has not just asked them to join with him as co-workers in his mission; he wants to take them to a new depth of union. This is contemplative knowing and living.

The mystics use language akin to a mystical marriage, to describe the deepest possible kind of union. It demands a complete surrender of the self and it is a response to the *holy longing* that many of them describe. I think we tend to hesitate a bit before this kind of intimacy. Jesus says we have to *die* for this to come about. Perhaps our work and activity becomes a protection from this kind of intimacy. None of us wants to

---

50 Matthew 16:13-17

give up the things of this world that we enjoy, but the mystics tell us that we can hold nothing back. Even our desire to be seen as spiritually successful, to be praised by others, to keep a good reputation, all this has to go in surrendering to the abyss of God's love. Even our images of God have to be given up since no image can adequately carry the mystery. Different mystics use different images for this journey of self-surrender, of *kenosis*, of emptying. Teresa of Avila describes the soul as an interior castle with different levels and rooms. John of the Cross speaks of the dark night of the soul. Meister Eckhart speaks of the virgin birth of God in the soul. For this to happen, whatever is not God has to be surrendered: the womb has to be virginal, the soul empty. Here we meet the coincidence of opposites: the poor have everything, the meek and humble inherit all there is; those who mourn are comforted; those who hunger and thirst are satisfied. One of the great modern theologians expressed these contradictions beautifully towards the end of his life:

> I have to accept the fact that my life is almost totally paradoxical. I have also had to learn gradually to get along without apologising for that fact, even to myself. It is in the paradox itself, the paradox which was and still is a source of insecurity that I have come to find the greatest security. I have become convinced that the very contradictions in my life are in some way signs of God's mercy to me.[51]

One winter morning I was sitting at a bay window overlooking Morecambe Bay. I was preaching an Advent retreat to the Augustinian Sisters at Boarbank Hall in Cumbria. I was praying the psalms of Morning Prayer. Looking up I saw that the winter sun had risen in a red ball over the water. I continued to pray. The next time I looked up there was also a small image of the sun reflected on the water. After praying some more I looked up again and the image had completely disappeared, burned up by the sun. I thought of those words of Thomas Merton, *As for me, all I want to do is to disappear into the face*

---

51 Karl Rahner Preface to *Poetry and the Christian* quoted in *Contemplation and Action* by Richard Rohr and Friends (Crossroad Publishing company NY 2006) p29

of God, and similar words of Meister Eckhart *between you and God there is no between.*

How can we achieve this? We cannot do this ourselves, it is the work of the Holy Spirit. What we can do however is adopt some form of regular practice. We have to make time for intimacy with the Lord, and it has to be a regular and daily part of our lives. We cannot make ourselves into contemplatives, but we can take away some of the blockages especially our chattering monkey minds, or our restless activities, and step into our inner room as Jesus recommends, where the Father is waiting for us in secret. The compassion, love and mercy we experience there is the compassion, love and mercy we can take into our care for others and for the world.

Chapter 11—Thomas Merton

Dogma and Doctrine, though necessary for the life of the Church, must always be open to the poetic God, the God whose word is heard in the stuttering and surprising language of the mystic.[52]

One of the reasons why there is a renewed interest in the contemplative stance today is because of Thomas Merton. Almost single-handedly, Merton rescued, for the Western Church, the lost teaching on silent prayer. Since my teenage years I have always been interested, even fascinated, by the figure of Thomas Merton. I would buy books such as *Seeds of Contemplation* and *Bread in the Wilderness*. I read the books, but I have to confess that I understood little of what Merton was saying. I looked in vain for any teaching about contemplation from priests, or religious educators; there was none available. I don't think I spoke to anyone about my interest in case they thought I was a bit odd. Later I discovered that many others were interested in Merton. His autobiography, published in America in 1948 as *The Seven Story Mountain*[53], was a bestseller. It was commended by Graham Greene and Bishop Fulton Sheen described it as a twentieth-century form of the *Confessions* of St Augustine. Since then his many books continue to be sold and read all over the world.

One of the attractions to me of Merton's writings is his honesty about the growth and development of his spiritual journey. Looking back, years later, on this famous bestseller he admitted that he would have said many things differently. He apologised to an Anglican woman who chided him for some very negative comments about Anglicanism. When in 1967 a high school student asked him how he might rewrite the book, Merton said he would cut out a lot of the sermons, and what he called the sales pitch for Catholic schools. The same is true of his other very popular early book *Seeds of Contemplation*. He later

---

52 Austin Smith, *Mersey Vespers* (Kevin Mayhew Ltd 2010) p13
53 UK title 1949 *Elected Silence*

published *New Seeds of Contemplation* which he described as almost a new book. It is this continued openness and willingness to search and learn that I find very attractive about Merton. This searching even took him on a remarkable journey to Asia in 1968 to meet and share with Hindus and Buddhists, including the Dalai Lama, at a time when dialogue with other religions was rare in Catholic circles. It was there that he met his death. He had been addressing a conference of Benedictine and Cistercian monks in Bangkok, Thailand, in December 1968, and was accidentally electrocuted in his hotel room due to a faulty fan and died instantly.

Merton's early life was troubled rather than settled. His mother died of cancer when he was just six years old; his father succumbed to the same disease, just thirteen days before his sixteenth birthday. He was a lonely but very intelligent student who won a place at Cambridge in 1933. This was a low point in his life, when despite his intellectual prowess his social life was spiralling out of control with heavy drinking and partying, including the fathering of a child. His guardian Tom Bennett took him back to the USA somewhat in disgrace. He enrolled at Columbia University and entered a period of stability and sanity.

Despite this early period of turbulence and meaninglessness there were moments in Merton's life when he seemed to be touched by God's grace. During his school days at Oakham in England, and on holidays in Scotland, he recalled his attraction to solitude in the hills. On a tourist trip to Rome, he was impressed by the art and mosaics in the churches, many of them portraying the figure of Christ. During that trip in 1933 he had a vivid dream that his dead father was present in his room and it led him to pray from the depths of his being.

In the calmer climate of Columbia, Merton started to read Catholic philosophers such as Jacques Maritain, poets such as Blake and Hopkins, and to share with his friends his idea of becoming a Catholic. The Catholic church of Corpus Christi was located just a few blocks away and one day as he read about Hopkins' own conversion story he got up, called in to Corpus Christi and began to receive instructions from Fr Moore. He was baptised on 16th November 1938.

On a personal note, I was privileged a few years ago to visit this church and to be graciously received by the pastor who showed me the baptistery where Merton was baptised, the Lady Altar where he made his profession of faith under the gaze of statues of two English saints, Thomas More and John Fisher, and the room in which he talked with Fr Moore. A year after becoming a Catholic, Merton asked to become a priest with the Franciscans and after being initially welcomed he suffered a painful rejection after he shared all the details of his past indiscretions in Cambridge.

Despite his crushing disappointment, he hadn't given up. He contacted the Trappists at Gethsemani Abbey, in the rolling hills of Kentucky. He made a Holy Week retreat there in spring 1941 and was deeply impressed with all that he saw and experienced. Returning to his teaching post at St Bonaventure University in Allegany, New York he prayed often to St Thérèse of Lisieux for guidance. One evening at her shrine in December 1941 as he prayed *show me what to do and I will be your priest* he vividly heard in his imagination the great bell of Gethsemani monastery. In *The Seventh Story Mountain* he recorded that *the bell was calling me home*. On the night of December 9th he was back in Kentucky and entered the place to which God had been leading him, to begin his life as a monk. He never expected to re-emerge: he was turning his back on the world. Fortunately, his superiors allowed him to write and, much later, to travel.

Given Merton's chequered past it's not surprising that his early years in the monastery coincided with a real rejection of the world he had left. Like St Augustine, before him, he was rather dismissive of anything the world had to offer. He described the movies he used to watch and the novels he had read as so much trash. He was becoming seriously pious, as happens with many new converts. He exhibited many of the characteristics of the first-half of life's spiritual journey: a search for identity and boundaries, a strong sense of moral obligation. In the first-half of life we try to give ourselves an ego structure; in the second half of life we have to let go of our egocentric life. This is a major surrendering of who we *think* we are. We have to let our nice self-image die, our desire to have a good reputation and to look good.

86

For Merton it meant becoming an observant monk and the dualistic spirituality of the time allowed him to slip into the easy judgement of religious life as good, life in the world as not so good. The danger for religious people is that the self-control developed in the first half of life all too easily leads to a sense of righteousness, and the judgements of the dualistic mind.

The key difference between the first and second half of life is the shift from religion as morality, trying to achieve personal perfection, to religion as mysticism, the shift from dualism to non-dual living. I don't think we ever get totally into non-dual living, but I think that we have to try to find a balance so that we don't get stuck at the dualistic level. We reach the second half of life usually by an experience of love, when our self-centred lives become other-centred; by some kind of suffering, and by suffering we mean something which we cannot fix or change. The third way into the second half of life is mysticism. Here we begin to taste the radical unity of all things and all people in God.

The way Merton talks of this journey is to speak about the false and the true self. The more Merton prayed and studied the Fathers of the Church, and reflected on the scriptures in his monastic life, the more he was articulating this crucial search for true identity, not one created for by our egocentric efforts, but already given to us as our true self in the centre of our being. This became a central theme in his many writings as a monk, and it exploded into his consciousness in a famous mystical experience which he had at a busy street corner in Louisville in 1958, which we will refer to later.

I think Merton's search for the true self was helped by all three pathways: love, suffering, and contemplative prayer. In the monastery his life was totally dedicated to the love of God, for whom he had given up everything that the world valued as important. On his ordination card he expressed the desire to disappear into God. But the early enthusiasm, peace and joy that he experienced eventually turned into suffering and darkness. He wrote to friends about a *disintegration of the spirit*. He was never in robust health and he found the primitive conditions of the monastery and the harsh diet difficult to deal with.

But it was the testing of both body and spirit that led him into what spiritual teachers describe as the dark night of the soul. Eventually the torment subsided and he began to feel peace and joy at a deep level of his soul.

Although he had turned his back on the world and his fellow men and women, Merton's contemplative experience of prayer was leading him to a new realisation that union with God did not lessen, but in fact deepened the sense of union with others. This insight was brought into his consciousness in an extraordinary way by what is called his *Louisville Vision*. He had travelled into the city to meet an editor and as he stood at the corner of an intersection on a busy Saturday afternoon, he had a mystical vision into the souls of ordinary people as they went about their business. All sense of separateness that he had felt about people living in the secular world faded away, all sense of specialness in his monastic vocation was absorbed into a deeper experience of non-duality. Afterwards he said that he now realised that the illusion of a separate holy existence was merely a dream. He now realised that there are no strangers. Some years later, reflecting on this experience, he said that this vision had revealed the secret beauty of people's hearts and it was so overwhelming that if we could only see each other in this way all the time, all wars would stop.

What Merton seemed to experience was something of the beauty of the true self. He continued to write about this theme in many of his writings. He was now exploring the second half of life's spiritual journey in which we discover the treasure within, in the core of our souls. The mystics tell us that we don't have to find God outside ourselves, but to awaken to the pearl of great price which is already given to us. This treasure, this pearl, is given to everyone; the only difference is that some people awaken to this mysterious presence and some don't. Our busy extroverted Western culture makes it very enticing to stay at the unaware level of the false self. The East, on the other hand, has kept alive the inner journey in its spirituality, and this is what inclined Merton to ask his superiors if he could travel to Asia and dialogue with other religious leaders, at a time when this kind of approach was very rare among Catholics.

Having moved out of his dualistic separation from others, Merton began to explore how the true self relates to ourselves, as well as to others, and to the world of creation. He sometimes refers to the true self as our *whole self,* in the sense that it reveals our true identity, our real identity. Merton also suggests that the true self is part of God because it is what makes us one with God. We are all, at this moment, being loved into existence by God. If that were not happening we would cease to exist, and that means that God's love is the reality of who we really are. We are God's love made manifest, the invisible made visible.

In the first half of life we learn doctrines and dogmas about God, we say prayers to God, and we try to behave morally to please God. In the second half of life, if we can move into contemplative experience we place ourselves before God in such a way that he can grant us a direct experience of his love and his presence. Then our attempts to live truly-loving lives flow from the deepest part of our being, not from our egocentric self, but from the love within. This is how the Martha and Mary story unfolds within us. We move from the autonomous action of the false self to a participation in the life and love of the Trinity. We are authentically real when we are loving.

The social dimension of this teaching is clear and radical. Although we are different from others, we are, nevertheless, deeply united to them in God, since we all flow into existence from the same source. That is why Merton can say that if we were really aware of this reality, war would cease to exist. In the second half of his journey, Merton started to write more and more about the social issues of his time and to engage with them. His topics included war, peace, racism, nuclear weapons. Sometimes his writings, in these areas, upset his superiors and censors. He had reached the level of contemplative oneness that breaks all boundaries of race, religion and culture. Contemplative experience is not genuine unless it awakens us to our fundamental unity. This sense of connectedness also includes the planet and the universe in which we find ourselves. Merton referred to this as the *cosmic dance.*

In *New Seeds of Contemplation* he writes:

> What is serious to men is often very trivial in the
> sight of God. What in God might appear to us as
> *play* is perhaps what he himself takes most
> seriously. At any rate the Lord plays and diverts
> Himself in the garden of his creation, and if we
> could let go of our own obsession with what we
> think is the meaning of it all, we might be able
> to hear His call and follow him in his mysterious
> cosmic dance.[54]

The false self, on the other hand, tends to take itself very seriously. It
sees itself as the centre of the universe and it lives more by non-
relating, by attitudes of fear, of negativity, of reactivity. While the
saints and the mystics look at reality as it really is, with a sense of
gratitude for the gift of everything that arises from the generosity of
God, the false self seeks to control and fix reality to fit into *my* limited
perspective. The true self can even look at experiences of suffering and
pain and transform them by taking them into the deepest centre of the
soul. Merton describes this as a point of pure nothingness which is also
pure truth, like a pure diamond, that belongs only to God and lies
beyond our disposal.

The true self also helps us to understand the true nature of the ego,
which is our self-reflective awareness of ourselves, including our
thoughts and our emotions. Our ego suggests that we possess
ourselves in our thoughts and emotions. *It's my life,* as we are
encouraged to shout these days. *This is my opinion and I've got every
right to it*, as we hear on the talk shows. Our ego expresses itself as,
I want, I feel, I remember, I think, I like, I don't like. Now since Merton
describes the true self as the *whole self* he would include the ego in all
of this. The ego then appears as the visible expression of our face to
the world. This is the concreteness of who we are. This is why we can
say that God wants us to have a healthy ego. It is the unhealthy ego
that has to *die* in the spiritual journey of the second half of life.

54 Thomas Merton *New Seeds of Contemplation* (New Directions NY 1972) p296

An unhealthy ego creates suffering both for ourselves and those who live with us. We live in the false self when we think that our ego is all that we are. It is the over-identification with our sense of separation from God, our lack of awareness that we are one with our true self, and therefore with God and with everyone else.

It is equally dangerous to think that we can live in the true self, in other words, live a holy life, without our egos. This is the trap of pious spirituality. If you think of a time when you have met someone who is genuinely holy, I think that what is evident is their ordinariness, their obvious humanity, their sense of humour about life and particularly about themselves. Their lack of agenda and concern about themselves is in fact the manifestation of a healthy ego integrated into the true self.

What attracts me to Merton is that many of those who met him spoke of his humanity, his warmth, his down-to-earth attitude. I referred, in Chapter Four, to the time when he said to James Finlay, *When you come to see me just tell me about the pigs. Tell me about each one of them. Tell me how they are.* Merton was teaching James Finlay about the mystery of presence. It's something he teaches all of us. For Merton the gate of heaven is everywhere.

Chapter 12—Julian of Norwich

In all eternity Jesus will never leave the position he takes in our soul; for in us is his most familiar home and his favourite dwelling.[55]

Thomas Merton died in 1968. Had he lived another five years he might have heard of an event in Norwich, England that would have interested him. It was a celebration in Norwich Cathedral to mark the 600th anniversary of Julian of Norwich. People came from many parts of the world to attend, but the people of Norwich were largely ignorant of the central figure being commemorated. Many of them asked, *Who is this man?* They did not realise that this person was not a man, but a woman. She had composed what many regard as the first book to be written in English by a female writer. Merton would have been well aware of this shadowy figure; he regarded her as the greatest of the English mystics.

We have few facts about Julian's life. It is generally assumed that this woman who lived in Norwich in the fourteenth century was married, and probably had at least one child. It seems that she lived through three outbreaks of the bubonic plague known as the Black Death which killed one third of the population of England, and may well have killed her own family. We have no proof of this, but what is beyond dispute is that Julian wrote a book that disappeared and remained unheard of until centuries after her death.

Scholars of Julian suggest that she was born in 1342 and died around 1420. The reason why 1973 was chosen for the commemorative event was because her book is a long meditation on events that Julian herself testifies occurred on 8th May 1373. In those days life was short and at the age of thirty she fell seriously ill. She had been bed-ridden for a week, in a lot of pain, and was apparently at the point of death. Benedicta Ward, in a lecture given in Norwich in 1988, suggested that at the time Julian was living as a widow with other members of her

---

55 Julian of Norwich *Revelations of Divine Love* (Penguin Classics London 1998 Ch 22) p33

family. The local priest was called to administer the last rites; but instead of dying, Julian experienced a profound mystical vision, which she recounts as her *showings*. The first of fifteen *showings* began early in the morning at around four o'clock and lasted until after the middle of the day. A sixteenth occurred on the following night. Julian had little doubt that these powerful experiences were from God so she set them down in her first and shorter account for the benefit of all Christians. Her meditations continued to be illumined for many years and a final *showing* took place around 1388. Julian concluded that the purpose of all these *showings* was entirely focussed on love, hence her desire to share her experiences with as many as possible.

After her recovery, Julian made a change of lifestyle and became what was known as an anchoress. In order to do that she would have had to convince the bishop that this was God's will for her. Permission was granted and after a ritual *burial service* was performed over her, she entered her cell which was attached to St Julian's Church in King Street, Norwich, hence the name by which she is now known. Her room would have had three windows: one which opened into the church through which she could see the tabernacle, the second would provide access for a maid to bring in food, and the third would open out to the street and be used by members of the public who would seek advice and counsel from the anchorite. This kind of vocation was common at the time and anchorites might have also served the community by teaching children or doing needlework for the church. Most of their time was spent in meditation and prayer. Julian's house was pulled down at the time of the English Reformation of Henry VIII, and St Julian's Church was destroyed in World War II. Both have since been restored.

At the beginning of her book Julian records how while she was still young she asked God for three gifts. One of these was to experience a serious illness at the age of thirty. This might seem a strange request but I think it expresses her intuitive grasp of the need to *lose life* as Jesus suggests in order truly *save it.* It was her way of entering the journey of the second half of life. She would be cleansed by the last rites and then be ready in the light of this illness to begin a new life more dedicated to God. Her second request was to have a vivid perception of Christ's passion. She wanted to know what it was like for Our Blessed Lady, Mary Magdalene, and the other women to be eye-witnesses of this event. Her third request was for the gift of three wounds: contrition, compassion and longing for God.

On the day of her anointing, after her parish priest had given her the last rites he left her with a crucifix to hold. As she gazed at it, the room went dark, while the crucifix remained bathed in light. Her breathing became more difficult and then suddenly, at around four o'clock, the pain left her and the *showings* began. They included a very direct experience of the passion of Jesus. In medieval piety it was not unusual to concentrate on the physical details of the passion. This is not so common today, but if we are to understand what Julian was asking for we have to reflect on the vexed question of sin. I say vexed because I think that the mystery of sin remains a big problem for many believers —and unbelievers too.

Too often we Christians have been burdened by a view of sin and the cross, rooted in the image of a vengeful God seeking to punish. This has left many with a heavy burden of guilt and shame which expresses a notion of God who seems to set impossibly high standards for us and then punishes us for failing to live up to them. In reality the cross is the great transformative mystery of the Christian faith: it is about God's forgiveness not his vengeance. It teaches us what to do with the great question of suffering and evil. The answer is to transform the evil and suffering into love. What were Mary, the other women, and John the beloved disciple doing at the foot of the cross? The answer lies in the mystery of love as participation. By their presence they were sharing Jesus' sufferings. What they teach us is that real love is impossible without vulnerability to pain and a desire to carry the burden of evil in our world, and so transform it.

What Julian learned in her *showings* was the underlying joy at the heart of the passion of Christ. This needs some explanation and it is one reason why Julian's book is so important for us today. Our secular world has rightly rejected the thought of a vengeful, vindictive God.

Religious believers need to do the same. As Julian was looking at the suffering of Jesus, instead of being sad, she is filled with great joy:

> And as part of the same showing the Trinity suddenly filled my heart with the greatest joy.[56]

God is not seeking satisfaction in the death of Jesus. He is showing us the infinite nature of his love and his forgiveness. Some of the passages of the Old Testament point to a god who requires sacrifices so as not to punish human beings. We thought we had to shed blood to get to God. The death of Jesus completely reverses this and shows us that it is God who sheds his blood to get to us. In doing this he pleads with us not to create any more victims. He breaks through our dualistic fear that sees the enemy as the problem. In Jesus we see total oneness with the Father and total oneness with everyone. This is the source of Julian's joy, while witnessing the sufferings of Jesus on the cross. Here again, as with all the mystics, we come across the mystery of paradox, the holding of tension between suffering and joy, light and dark, heaven and earth. Jesus hangs on the cross extending his arms to both the good and the bad thief, and they represent both parts of who we are, as Jesus reconciles all things.

Duns Scotus makes the point that Jesus did not become human as a mopping-up rescue mission type of exercise. The Incarnation is the highpoint of creation, the joining of matter and spirit. Jesus is and always was the primordial human being, the eternal word of God. What happens to Jesus is the pattern for all of us. His death is not the act of a vengeful God, but the death of all our fears and shame about our own humanity and that of others. We all come from God, we belong to God, and the death of Jesus shows us how to die to our egocentric, individual fear-bound existence, as we return to God in the glorified body of Christ. Julian saw that Jesus embraced the cross as an act of the most profound love to free us to become who we are created to be in him. Paul expressed it clearly to the Galatians, *I have been crucified with Christ; and it is no longer I who live, but it is Christ who lives in me.*[57]

---

56 Julian of Norwich *Revelations of Divine Love* (Penguin Classics London 1998 Ch 4) p46
57 Gal 2:19-20

Julian is therefore happy to share in the sufferings of Jesus so that she too can be transformed into him. In the next chapter of her *showings* Jesus demonstrates his infinite love for us and for everything created by showing her a tiny hazel-nut, round as a ball, in the palm of her hand. When she asks, *What can this be?* The answer is, *It is all that is made.* She hears how God creates such a tiny object, cares for it, and keeps it in being, all through love. This leads Julian not just to look upon created things with love but to desire to be totally united with the source of that love, which leads us to her third request of God.

While looking on the physical wounds of Jesus in the passion Julian desires three interior wounds. They are the wound of contrition, the wound of compassion and the wound of longing for God. While Julian's requests for a near-death experience, and a clear vision of Jesus' sufferings on the cross might appear beyond the normal Christian path, her third request is something we can all share. But we can ask why she refers to these gifts of contrition, compassion, and longing for God, as wounds?

There is plenty of scriptural evidence for use of the word *wound* in the spiritual journey. The whole people of Israel pass through the wounding experience of forty years in the Sinai desert; later they experience the years of exile in Babylon, not to mention the Roman occupation at the time of Jesus. Many of the mystics use the word to describe God's love as a wound in the soul. Wounding seems to be a powerful opening into transforming love, a love in which the egocentric self is broken open before the love of God:

> Through wounds, fissures in the self, God finds a way into us that is not possible when we are invulnerable, walled about, safe and secure. Wounds open up areas of the self that we would rather keep hidden. Wounds force us to confront our neediness and pain. But ultimately, for

Julian, the wounds of contrition, compassion, and longing, actually heal us.[58]

During the course of our lives all of us get wounded in some form or other. We are scarred by relationships that don't work out, or sickness or suffering; or children who disappoint us; we may experience loneliness; we may feel that our gifts have not been adequately recognised by others; or our health starts to deteriorate. Henri Nouwen wrote about the giftedness of the wounded healer. I recall a woman sharing with me the deep wounds of abuse she had experienced early in life. Despite the pain, maybe in and through the pain, she was now helping to heal others through her work. John of the Cross once remarked that the more wounded we are, the healthier we can become. Once again we are taken into the mystery and wisdom of paradox.

By asking for the wounds of contrition Julian does not intend wallowing in guilt. She does not expect us to spend time blaming ourselves. Our secular world might be right to turn away from religion as guilt, but there can be a flaw in rejecting authentic contrition, because it is part of our human condition. Genuine contrition softens our hearts. None of us are perfect, yet our modern media can be ruthless and vindictive in identifying wrong doers. We lapse, all too easily, into the game of scapegoating, which the passion of Christ tries to eliminate. Julian's emphasis on love and even joy in the mystery of the cross offers us a freedom which, to our modern world, seems threatening. Two thousand years after Jesus, we still seek our victims to blame and shame and dualistic religion often leads the way. Genuine contrition doesn't minimise evil but it shifts the template from self-centred judgments to the mercy and forgiveness of God, which includes everybody. Julian's request from God was for the gift of *true* contrition. Her *showings* reveal that God is incapable of anger. Our contrition is the other side not of God's punishment but of his mercy.

---

58 Elisabeth Ruth Obbard *Through Julian's Windows* (Canterbury Press Norwich, 2008) p25

What Julian learned in her *showings* is that far from wanting to punish us for our sins God can't wait to forgive us. All we have to do is to acknowledge our sins and failings. Hence the *act of contrition* as it is commonly described:

> And in spite of all this I saw truly that Our Lord was never angry and never will be angry, for he is God: goodness, life, truth, peace, love; and his loving kindness does not allow him to be angry, nor does his unity...God is the goodness that cannot be angry for he is nothing but goodness; our soul is united to him.[59]

Julian even goes so far as to say that God allows us to fall so that we can acknowledge our total dependence on his mercy, which is always available. By seeing and recognising our sin we are raised higher in heaven than ever before by the mercy of God. For Julian the fall and the forgiveness are *both* the mercy of God.

Her second wound was that of compassion which flows naturally from contrition experienced as mercy. Perhaps it was reading Julian of Norwich that inspired Thomas Merton's description of an encounter with the God within *as mercy within mercy within mercy*. The Hebrew word for compassion is *hesed* which means loving kindness. Julian's vision of the passion of Christ is the foundation of her compassion for all people and all things in creation. Healthy religion is all about transformation, and true compassion as empathy for the other is the compassion of Christ working within the soul.

> Yes, I saw as far as this—that Our Lord rejoices in the tribulations of his servants with pity and compassion.[60]

Compassion is how we experience the unconditional love of God. It is directed at the preciousness of our brokenness. Mystics, like Julian, know this from their own experience.

---

59 Julian of Norwich *Revelations of Divine Love* (Penguin Classics London 1998 Ch 46) p108
60 Julian of Norwich *Revelations of Divine Love* (Penguin Classics London 1998 Ch 28) p80

Her final request was for the wound of longing. Mystics are those in whom this unappeasable desire has been awakened. It is the one thing necessary, it burns within us and never goes away. It is the birth of a new kind of seeing and living that recognises the divine in everybody and everything. It is how we will enjoy eternity, but the mystics begin eternity now in this life. Julian of Norwich is one of those who teach us to recognise God in everything we see. Some people may draw back from the contemplative path; but the wound is always there, expressed through dissatisfaction or unhappiness in the events of life that the pursuit of money or activism cannot assuage. Julian's life shows us that our deepest human affliction is the denial of the truth that God is in love with us and seeks intimacy with us. Our deepest longing is always to receive and give love. There is no gap between our desire for God and God's desire for us. In the end, infinite love will always prevail; that is why Julian can proclaim: *And all shall be well, and all shall be well, and all manner of things shall be well.*

We learn from Julian's wounds that the struggle with God is always an unequal one. We think of our forgetfulness, our waywardness, our brokenness, our selfishness, as obstacles to God's love. These aspects of our broken humanity will keep God at a distance. What the mystics reveal is that it is our very brokenness, our waywardness, our infidelity that draws God to us. That is what Julian learned gazing at the suffering figure of Jesus who told her that he would do it over and over again to convince us of his loving mercy and forgiveness.

Chapter 13—Thérèse of Lisieux

St Thérèse in my view is the key figure in the recovery of the contemplative tradition of the gospel in our time—a process that is desperately needed in the Christian community and is only just beginning to take root. Thérèse manifests an extraordinary penetration into the heart of Jesus' teaching about the kingdom of God, as well as a precise programme for bringing it into daily life. She understood and participated profoundly in Jesus' experience of the Ultimate Reality as Abba, a tender and loving word for Father.[61]

For two days in September 2009 I witnessed an extraordinary event. It was the visit to Liverpool Catholic Cathedral of the relics of Thérèse of Lisieux. The British secular press had produced various articles writing dismissively about the Catholic fondness for the bones of the dead. For these journalists it was as if the message of the Protestant Reformation and the Enlightenment had been ignored. Words like *superstition* and *irrational* were bandied about. In fact, the fear of this kind of reaction had underpinned the decision of the English and Welsh hierarchy not to allow a visit of the relics some years previously. In reality, enormous crowds turned up to show respect and devotion to this remarkable young French saint. As part of the crowd in Liverpool, I can only say I was deeply moved not just by the numbers that came, but by the devotion and calm reverence of so many people, young and old, who were drawn by this event. Similar crowds were recorded at all the other places that received the relics in the UK, and in the light of the Reformation, it was especially significant that they were accepted into York Minster. They were also taken into Wormwood Scrubs prison in London. Similar large crowds have been recorded in the many countries that have received these relics. At a time when religion is reportedly in decline in the West, we need to

---

61 Thomas Keating *St Thérèse of Lisieux* (Lantern Books, NY 2001) p6

examine the remarkable appeal of this saint. What is so special about Thérèse?

The quote from Thomas Keating goes to the heart of her appeal. Her whole life is a testimony to the mystery of love which is the mystery of God. Thérèse was able to overcome the dualistic teaching of her day which was reinforced by the rigorous teaching of Jansenism. It was a strict and inflexible spirituality which discouraged frequent reception of the Eucharist in view of deep human unworthiness. Salvation could only be achieved with great difficulty and piety had to be focussed on this individualistic task. Although Thérèse broke through this restrictive and negative view of God, she seems to have been influenced by it to some degree. She was embarrassed and felt shame, for example about her body.

Thérèse Martin was born in Alençon, France, on January 2nd 1873, one of nine children but only five survived. Both her parents had thought of entering religious life before they married. The family was comfortably well off. Thérèse spoke of the almost dreamlike happiness of her life as a young girl; but there were plenty of shadows in that idyllic existence. Her mother died of cancer when she was only four and this great loss made her shy and suspicious of strangers; she was only really content and safe in the protective security of her home. When her *second mother*, her older sister Pauline, entered the convent when Thérèse was only nine her vulnerability and loneliness increased, but it helped to develop in her a very strong will. When her older sister, Marie, also entered the convent in 1886, Thérèse's own desire to enter grew stronger and that determined self-will was evident in overcoming several obstacles, not least her tender age. She entered Carmel in 1888, when she was just fifteen years old.

The thread that unites her life both inside and outside the convent was her burning desire to become a saint. Her way of achieving this took the conventional path of individual striving, but as her prayer-life and her self-knowledge deepened she realised that she could not succeed by her own efforts. Her genius was to discover what she called her *Little Way* which she presented as a new way of holiness. In fact what

God's grace had led her to intuitively grasp was the spirituality of imperfection. This has always been present in Judaeo-Christian spirituality, but more by way of a subtext rather than as mainstream. It certainly wasn't widely taught in Thérèse's time. The dualism that separates us from God inevitably leads to a spirituality of performance, effort and willpower to reach God. It is a spirituality of ascent. What Thérèse embraced was a spirituality of descent. She called it her *Little Way* and it contrasts with what we might call the big way of ascent. It is this spirituality of imperfection that allows Thérèse to speak to so many people today. Although she was living an enclosed life which seems at odds with the way of the modern world today, she taught that the *Little Way* can be lived anywhere and at any time. It is simply living with as much love as possible, whatever one's circumstances. For Thérèse it was simple: everything is grace.

One of her favourite parables was the story of the Pharisee and the Tax Collector. In Luke's account the parable is introduced by Jesus with an illuminating comment which is easily missed:

> He also told this parable to some who trusted in themselves that they were righteous and regarded others with contempt.[62]

The Pharisee rattles off his good deeds while the poor tax collector can only apologise for his unworthiness. In his conclusion, Jesus says this man went home closer to God, and in doing this Jesus is clearly underlining his preference for the spirituality of imperfection over the spirituality of perfection. Here he is aligning himself with the subtext of the Jewish tradition: that God always chooses the poor, the excluded one, the rejected, and the barren woman. The Christian tradition largely forgot this as it embraced the power of the Christianised Roman world, and we saw bishops standing next to monarchs and emperors. In Thérèse's time bishops in the French Church were still members of the aristocracy. While she loved the Church, her spiritual genius was attracted much more to the spirituality of imperfection. Thankfully the Church has now declared her to be a Doctor of the Church, and she is

---

62 Luke 18:9

the only uneducated person to have her wisdom recognised in such a way.

The first step in the spirituality of imperfection is powerlessness, a place of poverty and need before God. Instead of being able to rescue ourselves with our effort and willpower the saints and mystics invite us to open ourselves to the wonderful forgiving mystery of grace. Instead of keeping us from God, our brokenness becomes the actual place of encounter and acceptance. I know from my own experiences, when preaching about the mercy and forgiveness of God, that people often raise the question of God's justice. Thérèse takes this issue head on:

> What sweet joy it is to think that God is **just**— that is, that he takes into account our weakness, he knows perfectly the fragility of our nature. What should I be afraid of?[63]

The emphasis on the word **just** is her own.

Thérèse had a great love of the scriptures, even in days when the full reading wasn't encouraged, and she clearly discovered the truth of the words in the first letter of John, that *perfect love casts out fear*. Her whole life and spirituality can only be seen as a witness to God's infinite love:

> God is love and those who abide in love abide in God, and God abides in them. Love has been perfected among us in this: that we may have boldness on the day of judgement, as he is so are we in this world. There is no fear in love, but perfect love casts out fear; for fear has to do with punishment, and whoever fears has not reached perfection in love. We love because he first loved us.[64]

Unlike the other great Carmelite woman, Doctor of the Church, Teresa of Avila, Thérèse lived a different kind of mysticism. Ruth Burrows speaks of *lights on* and *lights off* mysticism. The great Spanish mystic

---

63 Thérèse of Lisieux *The Story Of A Soul* (Paraclete Press, Massachusetts 2006) p204
64 1 John 4:16-18

seemed to experience some extraordinary visions and ecstasies while her French Carmelite counterpart lived a more *lights off* mysticism; but there can be no doubting Thérèse's deep union with God. From an early age her soul was flooded with a deep desire for God's love and she describes her first communion as a kiss of love. It was a kind of fusion; two had become one.

At one level it is easy to dismiss Thérèse's spirituality as laced with a girlish romanticism. She clearly didn't appeal to the taste of the great twentieth century German theologian Karl Rahner. Underneath the flowery and sweet language, however, was a soul of extraordinary strength and determination. This was demonstrated early in her life in her famous meeting with Leo XIII in Rome, and her request to enter Carmel when she was under age. As she knelt before Leo XIII and he advised her to follow the advice of the superiors she placed her hands on his knees and told him that one word from him would resolve everything. He replied that she would enter if it was God's will. Thérèse still wanted more, but the papal guards touched her on the shoulders to remind her to rise and leave. She still didn't move and describes in her account that she had to be forcefully lifted by the guards and practically carried away, not without having received the Pope's personal blessing.

It was this steely determination that fuelled her desire to live a life of complete abandonment to God. The path, however, was far from easy, and involved a lot of suffering. Towards the end of her life, this suffering was intensely physical, as her fatal illness spread and the doctor's efforts just increased her pains. In her earlier years the suffering took the form of human relationships. For Thérèse it was complicated by the fact that her three sisters lived in the same convent. They had to guard against setting up a Martin family clique in the community. There were around twenty women in the community and a number of these Sisters had their own personal shortcomings such as extreme touchiness and lack of judgement. Avoiding the natural inclination to give them a wide berth, Thérèse would seek out these Sisters in recreation time. She helped a very difficult sister to get to the chapel each day despite her negative comments. Eventually this awkward sister was completely won over by Thérèse's charm.

Much worse trials were to come her way. Her devoted father whose devout spirituality so much shaped his daughter's, began to suffer hardening of the arteries and severe dementia. He started to lose his faculties and give the family money away. As he deteriorated, he had to be institutionalised in Caen. This was a bitter cross for Thérèse and her sisters, who were unable to offer him any help. It was a real crisis for Thérèse's idea of God. How could a loving God allow such a good devoted man to suffer such an embarrassing illness? In those days people had much less sympathy for those who suffered in this way. It led the sixteen-year-old to experience, early in life, the transformative mystery of suffering such as Job encountered. Her idea of God was being purified of any superficial romanticism and a much deeper faith emerged from this crucible of suffering. Like Julian of Norwich she grew to realise that this kind of pain can only be transformed by following the paschal journey of Jesus with loving acceptance.

Perhaps it was this suffering that led her to discover her new path to holiness, her *Little Way*. After her father's death in 1894 she began to use the word *abandonment* more frequently in her writings. Previously she had used it to refer to trials and tests; now she begins to see it as a source of deep joy. She was learning that everything that God allowed was tinged with mercy and grace. Her youthful idealistic wish to become a saint had reached a new level of maturity. Her concern and gaze was shifting from self-conscious living to Christ consciousness.

When her sister Celine entered the convent after her father's death, she brought with her a book of quotations from the Old Testament which she gave to Thérèse. Reading these passages led to her *eureka moment* to shed light on her struggles and her inability to realise her youthful desire to become a saint:

> I've told myself God wouldn't know how to inspire desires that can't be realised. So despite my littleness I can aspire to sainthood. To make myself bigger is impossible; I have to put up

with myself as I am with all my imperfections. But I want to seek the means of going to heaven by a little way that is very straight, very short, a completely new way.[65]

She then refers to an invention of her times: an elevator, what we today call an escalator, used in the homes of the rich to climb stairs. She scours the scriptures to find such an *elevator* and finds it in the book of Proverbs:

Let all who are *simple* come to my house.[66]

Claiming this simplicity for herself she then discovers these words of Isaiah:

As a mother comforts her child so I will comfort you, and you shall nurse and be carried on her arm and dandled on her knees.[67]

These texts confirmed her more mature understanding that she did not have to become a saint by her own egoic efforts, because God would do it in her. She was moving from control to abandonment and surrender. Now she understood the words of Jesus that we have to become like little children to enter into kingdom consciousness.

What led to this moment was a coming together of two great teachers in the spiritual life: suffering and love. She came to realise that even love involves suffering as she came to terms with the essential weakness of the human condition: the need to put up with her own imperfections. The mystics and saints all seem to discover at some point in their lives that the more deeply they enter the mystery of Christ, the thinner the line becomes between joy and suffering. Throughout her life, Thérèse expressed an extraordinary love for God. Yet, even with that burning desire, she was unable to overcome her faults and failings.

---

65 Thérèse of Lisieux *The Story Of A Soul* (Paraclete Press, Massachusetts 2006) p230
66 Proverbs 9:4
67 Isaiah 66:13,12

When we read the lives of the saints we often see them describing themselves as great sinners. This can be off-putting to ordinary believers because their lives seem so superior to ours in the practice of heroic virtue. It just seems to leave the rest of us caught in the revolving door of inadequacy. The key that unlocks this problem and the attraction of Thérèse's *Little Way* is to change our understanding of sin. Too often, in religious language, the notion of sin is used to blame, exclude or shame us, and because we don't like to carry this burden ourselves we look for someone else to blame and exclude. That is how the dualistic judging mind works. The fact of the matter is that we are all wounded and our Christian theology chose to name this wound as *original sin*. It hasn't proved to be the best expression because it implies culpability. What Thérèse discovered in her *Little Way* is that God does not blame us for this wound and weakness. In fact the very opposite is true. God loves us unconditionally precisely in our weakness and brokenness. She learned that our preciousness, our powerlessness to live up to our ideals, that weakness that Paul glorifies in, is what draws God to us because he is a God of both justice and mercy. Our sinful wound is not the problem; it is the way in.

This doesn't mean that we can sit back and wallow, as it were, in our woundedness, or go out to hurt others. To say that the wound is the way in, is to say that it is the gate we have to pass through, which represents the transformation from living the self-centred life of the false self, to living in the true self of Christ consciousness. This is not a painless journey because the ego hates to give up control, and the only way, as Jesus shows, is to walk the thin line between suffering as love, and love as suffering.

Thérèse exhibited a deep longing to be totally united with God. At the same time what we also see in her life is the great paradox that this enclosed Carmelite nun is completely open to the sufferings of others and to the suffering of the world. Her contemplation doesn't, in any way, take her out of the world; it thrusts her right back into it.

Reading St Paul's teaching on the body of Christ she wants to be every vocation in the Church, including the desire to be a priest and a missionary. Seeing that this is denied to her because of the vocation she has chosen to follow, she goes straight to the heart of the matter, the *heart* being the operative word. Her life is totally given over to love. Her vocation is love; she chooses to live in the heart of the Church, and therefore in the world, as love.

The entry of her relics into the Anglican cathedral of York Minster underlines the great gift that she is to Christian spirituality. Like Luther, she understood Paul's choice of grace over law. Like Paul, she knew that imperfection was an inescapable fact of the human condition, and like Paul she had penetrated deep into the heart of God's mercy in her life of prayer. It wasn't a prayer-life full of consolations; she had long gone beyond that. Nor was it perfect in performance: she spoke of her inability to keep awake. But it had reached depths where she had experienced the mercy of God in a truly transforming way. Her *Little Way* had placed her firmly inside the bigger story of God's grace.

Her opening of herself to God's love at this deep level enabled her to unite contemplation and action. She was overjoyed when Mother Prioress asked her to adopt two missionary priests as her *brothers*. She could now live her missionary and priestly vocation through them. Her *Little Way* led her to do every action out of love, and allow even her failures to be transformed into love by the grace of God. She once remarked that even if she had every possible sin on her conscience she would never lose her confidence in God's mercy: she would throw herself into his arms and beg forgiveness. She could say this because she had met God as Abba in the core of her being. Thomas Keating underlines the profound truth that she had grasped about the mercy of God.

> This is one of the greatest insights of all time into the nature of God and our relationship with him.[68]

When as a fourteen-year-old Thérèse was being carried away by the Swiss guards from the presence of the Pope in Rome she couldn't have

---

68 Thomas Keating *St Thérèse of Lisieux* (Lantern Books,NY,2001) p36

dreamt that one day the Pope of Rome, John Paul II, would come on pilgrimage to her convent in Lisieux, and a few years later this same Pope would declare her, *Little Thérèse,* a Doctor of the Church. As she was dying she said that she would spend her heaven doing good on earth. The relics of this would-be missionary have drawn large crowds in over forty countries. It still goes on. When her cause was being discussed in Rome one of the investigators asked her sister, Pauline, what would be the purpose of canonising Thérèse. Her sister answered that it would teach the world about the mercy of God. The vast crowds who honour her relics seem to have grasped that.

Chapter 14—Bede Griffiths

All our conflicts arise because we stop at a certain level. Christians stop at the Christian religion, Muslims at Islam, and if you are a Hindu you stop at your own symbolism. Each one feels himself separate from the others. Only when you go beyond these distinctions and are open to the reality beyond, can you overcome these conflicts. The ultimate reality contains all the differences in the world. It does not abolish them. You and I are all contained in the Absolute. We see everything separated, but if you have the vision of reality, you perceive all the differences in that total unity.[69]

When I lived in the Salesian community in Bolton, Lancashire, I joined the local inter-faith council composed of Christians, Muslims and Hindus. One day, I walked down to the barber's shop and stood waiting for it to open after lunch. A Muslim member of the inter-faith council walked by and we chatted for a few minutes before he moved on. Later another man stood alongside me. He spoke about his reluctance to buy bread from the large supermarket across the street. I mentioned that there were several small shops along the road where he could get bread. *I know,* he replied, *but they are all owned by them.* I'm sure he wasn't a bad man, but his outlook represents one of the tribal and deep-seated expressions of dualism we find in our world today as we witness so much conflict and violence, often fuelled by religious or racial differences.

It is these conflicts that turn so many people away from religion: either they give up completely or they prefer to call themselves *spiritual* rather than *religious.* I'm told that 22% of the population of the USA describe themselves in such a way. This is unfortunate because, for all

---

69 Bede Griffiths, *The Universal Christ,* Daily Readings edited by Peter Spink (Darton, Longman & Todd, London 1990) p50

its faults, religion is the best way to overcome the separation of the individualistic self from the Ultimate Reality that we call God. The fact that so many people in the Western world don't see this is the reason why all religions need to reform themselves from time to time. That is essentially what Jesus was trying to do with the Jewish religion of his time. We face the same task today and one of the ways to do this is to move beyond the dualistic judgements of the mind and into silent prayer. This doesn't mean that we reject the wonderful achievements of the mind; what it calls for is an integration of our intelligence and knowledge as we move to a higher level of wisdom that can hold opposites together and help reconcile them.

Each religion has its own story which includes rituals, doctrines and moral behaviours. Today, more than ever, as we live our own stories and meaning patterns, we must, at the same time, respect each and every other story. Clearly there are obvious differences between them but the contemplative path is the way to a new sense of unity. This path leads us beyond our divisions to a deeper place of unity where we can experience love, compassion, and reconciliation. For Catholics, the Vatican Council document *Nostra Aetate*[70] opened this way to unity at the deepest level of who we all are in God. At present the religions of the world have not really grasped the urgency of this task but there are some prophetic figures who are pointing the way to the future. One of these is Bede Griffiths.

He was born Alan Richard Griffiths in Walton-on-Thames, England, in 1906, the youngest of four children. His family were respectable middle-class members of the Church of England, but he received little religious instruction from them. He grew up with an inquiring mind and his love for the mystery of nature and of life was fed by the works of Thomas Hardy and his interest in classical Greek tragedy. During his last year at school, he had a profound mystical experience while out walking in the country at sunset. His senses became acutely sharpened as he heard bird song with a new clarity. He was overwhelmed by the

---

70 *Nostra Aetate (In our Age)* is the Declaration of the Second Vatican Council on the Relation of the Church with Non-Christian Religions, promulgated on October 28, 1965, by Pope Paul VI.

setting sun, the sight of a hawthorn tree, a lark singing in the distance and the mystery of twilight. He felt a profound sense of awe in Rudolph Otto's sense of the word, the *mysterium tremendum*. He often described it as one of the key moments of his life and it opened him to the presence of the divine in the mystery of the cosmos.

Shortly after this experience he went up to Oxford and began to steep himself in the classics and the writings of Wordsworth, Keats, Shelley, and Blake, from whom he picked up the reference to *The Golden String*, which he would use as the title of his spiritual autobiography. His mentor was C S Lewis, who had by then cast aside the atheism of his youth in favour of a more mystical understanding. Lewis' life, surprised by the joy of an unexpected love and shattered by its painful loss through death, was brought to the world by the 1993 biographical film, *Shadowlands*, directed by Richard Attenborough.

Gradually Griffiths was led by the writings of St Paul into the mystery of a loving God and a search for meaning that led him into the Catholic Church in 1931. A year later he entered a Benedictine monastery where he was given the name Bede. Over the next twenty years he lived the conventional life of a monk, leading communities in both France and Scotland. By the 1950s he was beginning to express his dissatisfaction with the predominantly masculine and rational structure of Western monastic life. He felt that it wasn't really touching the needs of many spiritual seekers, and he began to explore the riches of Eastern spiritualities. To further this search he transferred to a Benedictine monastery in India in 1955, where he could begin to explore the more feminine, artistic and intuitive aspects of the spiritual journey. He described it as searching for the other half of his soul. He lived there until his death in 1993.

From this point on, his life can be summed up as an attempted marriage of East and West, a union of the masculine and the feminine, as he embraced the contemplative path into the mystery of God which all religions teach. From his ashram in Kerala he offered advice and counsel to all kinds of spiritual seekers. While recognising and respecting the different externals of each religion, he sought the unifying features of them all.

He wasn't trying to create a universal soup that contained all religions. He fully recognised and respected the many and varied differences that separates the different faiths. He wanted to move to a different level of consciousness that didn't reject intellectual and rational argument, but saw it as a necessary stepping stone to a deeper and more universal level of consciousness. He realised that if we remain at the level of rational, analytical awareness, we will not escape the situations of conflict and division that exist today.

More people are beginning to recognise Jesus as a wisdom teacher who is trying to lead us into non-duality. His own relationship to Ultimate Reality is described in the most intimate terms: *Abba, Father.* Jesus prays, in John's gospel, that all people will be one as he and the Father are one. This is a non-dual relationship. They are not two and they are not one. That is the nature of love. When you love somebody completely, you give yourself to them. You become one, yet you remain two; you are two, yet you become one. That is non-duality. You do not lose yourself in love, you truly find yourself. Jesus takes this further when he prays that this unity that he experiences with the Father will be enjoyed by all of us, *so that they may be one, as we are one, I in them and you in me.*[71] What happens in contemplative prayer is that we seek to enter into Christ consciousness, his intimacy with the Father, and this relational love between Father and Son is the Holy Spirit. For the Christian, ultimate reality is a communion of love characterised by mutual giving and receiving. According to Bede Griffiths, this community of love at the heart of God is unique to Christianity.

After being somewhat dismissive of science in his earlier writings, Bede learned to embrace the new discoveries of quantum physics as they reveal more and more of the mysterious connections in all created reality, while recognising that there is so much that we do not know.

---

71 John 17:22-23

In a recent series by BBC television on the wonders of the universe Professor Brian Cox remarked that what excited him most as a scientist is to stand on the threshold between the known and the unknown. This is the kind of language that the mystics have always used. Recall Julian of Norwich seeing everything contained in a hazelnut, and Meister Eckhart's and Hildegard of Bingen's stress on the human need for receptivity before the mystery. This is what motivated Bede's lifetime search into the mystery of God. Alongside theologians like Thomas Aquinas and John of the Cross, he realised that the ultimate mystery cannot be attained by human reason, and what we don't know will always be greater than what we do know.

The Christian understanding of the mystery sees creation as the Word of God and in that Word is contained every created thing, including the human soul. This is the great *I Amness*—the gift of being that we all share in God. Bede sees the Judaeo-Christian story of The Fall as the explanation for our separation from this unity of being:

> The Fall is our fall into this present mode of consciousness, where everything is divided, centred on itself and set in conflict with others. The Fall is the fall into self-consciousness, that is into a consciousness centred in the self which has lost touch with the eternal Ground of consciousness, which is the true self.[72]

Bede is not saying that self-consciousness is evil, but the task of the spiritual life is to die to that small self and rise into the larger true self that is the divine presence within. Sin is, therefore, the failure to do this: it is to miss the mark. Redemption is our transformation into what we might call *at-one-ment* with the risen Christ. The whole purpose of creation is the evolution of matter into consciousness. We are the universe made conscious. God's plan is to unite everything in heaven and earth into the Christ Self. The Word of God took on our human nature in all its frailty and poverty so that it can be transformed into

---

72 Bede Griffiths *Return to the Centre* (Medio Media, London 2003) p21

the divine. This is the treasure within, the pearl of great price, that all of us carry.

Much of our Westernised Christianity fails to teach this message. We have reduced spirituality to an individual struggle for private salvation. Our seminaries and programmes for priests and religious emphasise formation rather than transformation. We are still heavily influenced by the masculine model, which stresses rules, hierarchy, correct performance of ritual, vocal prayer, effort and willpower. Bede Griffiths saw the need to balance this with the more feminine, intuitive mind which embraces the contemplative path. Like Thomas Merton, he realised that we had much to learn from the religions of the East. He related how many in India would admire the charitable work and organisation of the Western Church; but they pointed to the lack of the inner journey. It is always a question of putting the two together, action and contemplation, and Bede wrote about this in his book, *The Marriage of East and West.*

He went to India, not so much to search for new ideas, but to seek a more integrated way of living. Like all visitors he was shocked by the poverty, but at the same time he was struck by the grace, beauty and vitality of the people. Throughout India, he discovered the awareness of the sacredness of everything. They hadn't experienced the split between sacred and secular that I wrote about in chapter four. They had retained the sense of cosmic unity in all things. Wonder and enchantment were normal experiences, not exceptional ones. As religious practice declines in the West, Bede argued in *Return to the Centre,* a more contemplative practice will help us to move out of our rational minds to that deeper place where we encounter, in our poverty, the treasure within. This leads us to the place of mystery beyond all words, concepts and images that the mystics point to as our destiny. A regular daily contemplative practice helps, like nothing else, to uncover the often egotistic motivations that hide in our activities, even religious ones. Bede taught that if we could learn to live from that centre we would live from the heart which sees everything as one, and live from our true self that is always one with God in love. This is the Great Compassion which resolves all sense of separation.

One of the highlights of Thomas Merton's Asian journey in 1968 was his meeting with the Dalai Lama whom Merton described as alert, energetic, simple and outgoing. The two men discussed different forms of prayer and got on very well. Bede Griffiths met the Tibetan leader in Australia in 1992 when they were both involved in lecture tours. They had met previously and the Dalai Lama greeted him warmly and affectionately, teasing him about his long white beard. They spoke about meditation and the Tibetan elders were impressed with Bede's grasp of high levels of Buddhist meditative practice. At the end of the conversation, one of the elders approached Bede, grasped both his hands and said, *Father, you are a very great man*. Both Bede Griffiths and Thomas Merton were genuine spiritual searchers who, while living and respecting their own Catholic Christian tradition, were prepared to dialogue with other faiths and seek the common goal and experience of the Great Mystery.

Bede Griffiths always said that he went to India to find the other half of his soul. There can be no doubt that he found it. He relates how when he was meditating in his ashram, on the morning of 25th January 1990, he was struck by a terrific force, like a sledgehammer, as he later described it. It knocked him out of his chair, although he managed to crawl back into his bed where he did not move or speak for a week. One night he recovered consciousness and felt he was about to die, but nothing happened. Like Julian of Norwich he then experienced a mystical experience. He heard an inner voice saying, *Surrender to the mother*. He told his friends later that at that moment he was overwhelmed by love. One of his friends, who was present by his bed, recalled that he said the words, *I am being overwhelmed by love*. He had an image of the Black Madonna, as the mother of both earth and heavens.

This experience remained with him and it moved him beyond the duality that is our *normal* way of seeing. He saw all divisions breaking down as everything flowed into everything else. It was not that all divisions disappeared but he saw the underlying unity in everything and everybody. For the remaining three years of his life, Bede taught the great relational mystery of the Trinity. Everything springs forth from the Father, the Ground of all being, and from that boundless abyss comes forth the Word, the eternal expression of the Father's love. In the Incarnation all created beings are revealed as touched by the divine. At the time of the Big Bang the creative power of God is manifested in space and time and continues to evolve in matter and spirit. This energy of the Spirit is what inspires everything in creation.

For Bede, this creative energy is an expression of the feminine, and in our times this healing power of the feminine is becoming more evident to counteract the excessive patriarchal bias of our world. This task of integrating the masculine and the feminine is one of the greatest challenges of our times. Not only must we try to do this to save our planet from destruction, but we must also integrate the masculine and the feminine in our own souls. This is where the active and contemplative paths merge as one path. We have long been accustomed in our present understanding to use only masculine words to speak of God. We know that none of our words and concepts can fully contain the awesome mystery of God; but spiritual voices are freeing us to embrace both masculine and feminine language to explore the mystery.

Both Julian of Norwich and Thérèse of Lisieux spoke of the motherhood of God. Merton too, towards the end of his life, seemed to achieve this integration especially in his prose poem *Hagia Sophia* in which he wrote of an invisible fecundity, a hidden wholeness in all things which he called his sister, Wisdom. Carl Jung claimed that there could be no real mystical union with God without some integration of the masculine *animus* with the feminine *anima*.

This task is perhaps one of the most difficult spiritual challenges of our time. Whatever theological, catechetical or pastoral renewal programmes are being explored, we have to heal the split between male and female. We are being challenged to bring the feminine qualities of mystery, gentleness, intuition, sensitivity, compassion, receptivity and reverence for the earth. These relational qualities have to be merged with the masculine drive for order, control, clarity, analysis, and organisation. We need both *Brother Sun* and *Sister Moon*.

Chapter 15—John O'Donohue

There is a quiet light that shines in every heart. It draws no attention to itself though it is always secretly there. It is what illuminates our minds to see beauty, our desire to seek possibility and our hearts to love life. Without this subtle quickening our days would be empty and wearisome, and no horizon would ever awaken our longing. Our passion for life is quietly sustained from somewhere in us that is wedded to the energy and excitement of life.[73]

We are caught between two siren voices. The voice of the secular world leads us down the ever-narrowing horizon of a world bereft of the sacred. The infinite longings of our hearts are reduced to trying to *make it* in this world. *If you can make it here you can make it anywhere,* the denizens of New York City used to proclaim loudly. Like Adam and Eve, we seek to be our own gods, and to secure our happiness by endless consumption, by competition, by seeking power over others, by shoring up our egotistic world view. Like the inhabitants of Plato's cave, transfixed by the flickering shadows on the walls, unaware of the sacred world outside. The task of healthy religion and spirituality is to lead us out of the narrow cave into the infinite mystery beyond. Sadly, today, religion is not often perceived this way. It struggles to connect the outer and the inner journey. It leaves us stuck in a largely dualistic world view that affirms the sacred, but nonetheless leaves it divided from the secular. We seem to be telling half a story to a world that is hungering for a more expansive and exciting plot. The religious voice is pointing to God; while forgetting the human. The secular voice points to the human, and forgets God. We seem to fear the mixing of ordinary and extraordinary that is the Incarnation.

---

73 John O'Donohue *Benedictus* (Bantam Press London,2007) p14

Of the five people I have written about in part two, John O'Donohue is the only one I was privileged to meet. With two Salesian friends I attended an Advent reflection weekend which he led. It was a bit like an Emmaus experience as our hearts burned within us listening to his wisdom, but I also remember his very hearty laugh. John loved life and loved people. If Bede Griffiths travelled to India to find the other half of his soul, I think that John O'Donohue found it in the landscapes of his native West of Ireland where he learned to love the air, the stones, the flowers and the sea. He lived in a remote cottage until his untimely death in January 2008, while on a speaking engagement in France.

John was born on New Years' Day in 1956 in County Clare, one of four children. He grew up in The Burren, a rather stony place of wild beauty. He seemed to get his mystical bent from his father, and both father and uncle taught him a love for poetry, language and music. Like many young boys in Ireland, at that time, he was drawn to the priesthood. So, after his early education at St Mary's College, Galway, he went on to study philosophy and theology at St Patrick's, Maynooth and he was ordained in 1981. He served as a parish priest in both Clare and Connemara[74] and studied for his doctorate on Friedrich Hegel for four years at Tubingen University in Germany. The urge to write both prose and poetry grew in him, but sadly his superiors wanted him to remain in full-time parish ministry.

John found this restriction increasingly irksome, coupled with what he perceived to be a lack of vision in Church leaders and their inability to appreciate the feminine. Sadly, he came to the painful decision to leave the priesthood. In one sense he never left it: he said that the best decision he ever made was to become a priest; the second best decision was to leave the priesthood. Free of the day-to-day claims of parochial ministry, his poetic and philosophical spirit was able to reflect on and communicate the more mystical tradition of the Church which is not often fed by traditional parish ministry. His first book *Anam Cara*, on the subject of soul friendship, became a best seller, to be followed by other writings: *Eternal Echoes, Divine Beauty, Benedictus,* and a

---

74 *Connemara* is the English spelling for *Conamara*.

book of poetry, *Conamara Blues*. His themes of presence, belonging, friendship, memory, blessing, and a fascination with the changing landscapes of the West of Ireland, were rooted in the Celtic tradition which is one part of the Western Church that has remained more in touch with the contemplative pattern of life.

He wanted to move away from the moralistic straightjacket that restricted the spiritual journey to a set of rules to be obeyed and doctrines to give assent to. He sought to invite his readers to make the adventurous inner journey into their souls, to find the treasure within, and so look on the outer world with new and contemplative eyes. For him, the narrow gate into this kingdom of God is an awareness of the presence of Beauty, as the place where the visible and invisible worlds meet. If we can enter this narrow gate it opens up the vast spaciousness of infinite beauty that graces everything in creation. For John O'Donohue this is a pressing need in our contemporary world, which has lost its sense of the sacred mystery of life.

Today we appear to have lost the language of respect for what the mystics call *Otherness*. We still don't know how to live, in our shrinking planet, with respect for difference and so often we choose violence as a means of solving problems. We don't seem to know how to talk to each other. We are trapped in the dualism of difference, unable to see what we have in common. That is why the language of the mystics is so important. The search for beauty, truth and goodness was the ancient way to wisdom, and we need prophetic voices today to help us articulate these deep needs of the human heart and spirit.

The great journey of the twentieth century was into outer space; the great adventure of the twenty-first century will be the inner journey to find our heart and souls. Spirituality has to produce pathfinders who can encourage others to follow this new consciousness. For John O'Donohue the journey is essentially one of homecoming to who we are in God:

> The human soul is hungry for beauty; we seek it everywhere—in landscape, music, art, clothes, furniture, gardening, companionship, love,

religion, and in ourselves. No-one would desire not to be beautiful. When we experience the Beautiful there is a sense of homecoming.[75]

John O'Donohue argued that all our contemporary crises can be reduced to a crisis about the nature of beauty. Our media has elevated glamour and celebrity above the need to love beauty. Celebrities have become the new priesthood in our times with their views and opinions filling talk shows and magazines. So many lives, especially the young, are caught up in the desire to dress like and imitate the rich and famous. Contrast this media-driven frenzy with the vision of Thomas Merton in Louisville, Kentucky, when he saw the beauty and glory of people's souls. The media culture is essentially dualistic: a favoured few have glamour and fame; the rest of us do not. It creates envy and unhappiness, a restlessness of spirit. Centuries ago, Augustine pointed to this inner restlessness as a sickness of the human spirit, and bemoaned his own late discovery of the treasure within. This is what Jesus came to teach us: that the pure of heart shall see the divine, taste the mystery, be surprised by the sacred beauty all around us. For Jesus it's not wealth and fame we need but eyes to see and ears to hear.

We tend to think of beauty as something special, associated with the extraordinary. We reduce spiritual transformation to endless serenity, contentment, a sense of completion. Nothing could be further from the truth. Think of the suffering of Thérèse of Lisieux and so many of the saints and mystics. This is one of the problems of the growing split between religion and spirituality. The spiritual search can easily become an individualistic search for peace and nirvana, untouched by the problems of the world. That is a spirituality that simply feeds the ego. Authentic spirituality needs religion, community, doctrines, ritual, ethical behaviour, care for the poor and disadvantaged, as much as religion needs a spirituality that feeds the longing of the soul for the abiding presence of the divine.

---

75 John O'Donohue *Divine Beauty* (Bantam Press London 2003) p2

Living in the wild landscapes of Connemara, John O'Donohue was fully aware of the deep longings of the human spirit, of the fact that spirituality is not so much about contentment as learning how to live with our discontent. This is the spirituality of unknowing, of longing for something better, of something more, of being prepared to face the deeper questions of the heart:

> When we devote no time to the inner life, we lose the habit of soul. We become accustomed to keeping things at surface level. The deeper questions about who we are and what we are here for visit us less and less. If we allow time for soul, we will come to sense its dark and luminous depth. If we fail to acquaint ourselves with soul, we will remain strangers in our own lives.[76]

Like all the mystics, John felt the need for reverence before the mystery of life, its light and its dark moments, its joys and the sorrows, its moments of illumination and also of darkness.

If we can accept Jesus as a wisdom teacher then it becomes clearer how he *saves* our world. Too often salvation is seen as saving our individualistic souls for eternal life in heaven. What Jesus teaches us is how to taste this different kind of life, that we call eternal life, right now in the midst of ordinary life. The gospels reveal this new way of life in the resurrection appearances of Jesus, to Mary Magdalene and the disciples. A common feature to all of them is the recognition problem. They don't initially recognise Jesus; he seems different, yet it really is him. His presence seems to be physical but goes beyond the physical in a more subtle form. He eats fish and shows his wounds to Thomas; yet he is able to appear in a locked room, and he asks Mary Magdalene not to cling to him. Nor does he want the two disciples on the way to Emmaus to remain trapped in the story of the past. Jesus is trying to get his followers to move into the future when his presence will be more spiritual rather than physical. That is why he goes before

---

76 John O'Donohue *Divine Beauty* (Bantam Press, London 2003) p39

them into Galilee. They knew him as Jesus of Nazareth; now he will be known as Jesus the Christ, available and present in all of creation and to all people.

It is this borderline of presence and absence that the mystics and saints inhabit and invite us to share. They point not so much to eternal life in heaven but to the eternal now. The message of the Incarnation is that God's love is revealed by Jesus as embracing the limitations of the human condition. He accepted humanity as it was, not as it should be. We all like to experience joy and happiness, peace and tranquillity in our lives, but experiences like pain, suffering, hatred and aggression keep getting in the way. Our tendency is to *fix* these situations from the outside by some external intervention, and to get angry with God when we can't fix them. In his life and death, Jesus chose to reject this kind of power in favour of powerlessness. This is so counter-intuitive for us. We think that we are here to change the world, and to some extent this is true, but Jesus teaches us that sometimes we have to enter into the suffering and the pain, feel it to its depths as it were, as he does in Gethsemane and hold it in the embrace of love. Holiness is holding the tension of opposites.

If we are to present an authentic spirituality for the times in which we live we have to learn to live with and hold this tension in the coincidence of opposites. We have to model an incarnational spirituality that reveals God as the great reconciler of all humanity, who draws all things to himself. Jesus did not come into this world to heal it from outside, bringing his divine power to every difficult situation. He tells Peter to put his sword away, as his enemies come to arrest him. He had lived his life fearlessly speaking out against the oppression of the poor, but he was also prepared to take the consequences as the religious and political forces sought to kill him. He remained vulnerable to the end and it was from that place of woundedness that he was raised from the dead.

I am always struck by the fact that the risen glorified body of Jesus is a wounded body. John O'Donohue writes movingly about this gift of woundedness, and sees it as the place where compassion is born.

It seems to be an essential ingredient in the shaping of a compassionate human heart that can enter, like Jesus does, into suffering and pain in a transformative way. For O'Donohue the greatest evil and destruction arises when people are unable to feel compassion.

To be able to hold the opposites together requires a firm rootedness in our identity as daughters and sons of God. At the same time, it requires an ability to create warm human friendships. Jesus certainly models this way of life with friends like Mary Magdalene, Martha, Lazarus, Peter, James and John and the other apostles and the women who accompanied him on his journeys. Many of the saints were noted for intimate friendships, such as Bernard of Clairvaux and the Duchess of Lorraine, Francis of Assisi and Clare, Philip Neri and Catherine of Ricci, Vincent de Paul and Louise de Marillac, Francis of Sales and Jane Frances de Chantal. Unfortunately this tradition of friendship became a victim of the rather disembodied spirituality and negative view of sexuality of recent centuries. Today it is being revived, and John O'Donohue's book *Anam Cara* has helped greatly in this necessary revival. For him when people love and allow themselves to be loved they participate in the kingdom of the eternal.

Friendship is rooted in vision. We all want to be seen, recognised and accepted. The love of friendship waters our souls and brings them alive to God's goodness imprinted within. It is a gift of true consciousness and awareness of the inner beauty of our souls. C S Lewis wrote a novel entitled *People Have Faces* in which he suggested that God is trying to create our faces as expressions of our souls. Friends too can do this. John O'Donohue rightly claims that when you look into someone's face you are looking into their soul. He writes of the rich privilege of having friends who pray for us each day even without us knowing about it, whose love enables us to face the loneliness and challenges of life. Such friends are for him not a luxury but a necessity.

The longing that friendship awakens is a hint of our deeper longing that only God can satisfy. God is not outside us; he lies within waiting to be discovered. The tenderness of friendship enables us to embark on this search with confidence. Once we have discovered this treasure within, we are no longer threatened by the dismissive glance of the dualistic mind. O'Donohue contrasts the intimacy and warmth of a loving gaze compared with the judgmental stare.

Healthy friendships allow us to embrace and forgive not just the woundedness and the limitations of others, but also our own failings and shortcomings. I think it is a danger for many generous Christians, including priests and religious, who are trained to serve others that they may all too often end up neglecting themselves. As a Salesian priest, I have been brought up to care for others, especially the young, the needy and the poor, those who may not have received enough parental love to feel secure about themselves, but I also need to be reminded sometimes to be a loving parent to myself.

As people live longer today, John O'Donohue reminds us of the danger of marginalising the elderly:

> I know some very old people who have hearts full of roguery, devilment and fun; there is a sparkle in their presence. When you meet them, you have a sense of light, lightness and gaiety. Sometimes in very old bodies there are incredibly young, wild souls looking out at you.[77]

From my own experience, as Rector of one of our elderly Salesian communities, I know for myself the truth of those words. One most-respected and valued friend of mine was ninety-eight years of age when he died. It was a community where we laughed a lot; as is true of the community in which I presently live. O'Donohue bases his comment on the profound insight of the mystic Meister Eckhart who stated that despite the aging of our bodies there is a part of our soul that is eternally young. What a consoling thought for all of us!

As I listened to John O'Donohue speak, on that Advent weekend a few years ago, it was interesting to note how many of his stories came from his time as a priest, and in particular his experiences with the dying. He referred to the fine Irish tradition of saying the rosary at the bedside

---

77 John O'Donohue *Anam Cara* (Bantam Press London 1999) p230

of the dying, but recalled how sometimes this repetitive prayer could get in the way of something more important. When the group of parishioners reached the end of a decade of the rosary, and before starting another, he would ask them to go outside and leave the family alone with the dying person. He would advise them to use those precious sacred moments as their mother/father/loved-one lay on the edge of eternity to tell them everything in their hearts that they wanted to say, so they would have no unsaid regrets.

Conclusion

I have dedicated this book to Damien, a neglected child who lived for a mere three weeks. I recalled how baptising this child was a very moving experience for me. My heart was touched by the tiny heart of this fragile baby. I have tried to describe the treasure which all of us carries within our hearts, the image and likeness of God. I don't think that Jesus came on earth to burden us with rules and regulations, although they have their place. He came to share the great adventure of what it is to be a human being, to invite us to participate in the great mystery of giving and receiving love that is the mystery of the Trinity. The mystics tell us that we don't initiate this mystery; it is an invitation to participate in the great dance of creation. As Thomas Merton says, it is never far away; it beats in our very blood whether we want it to or not.

Michael

Other books by Fr Michael J Cunningham SDB

Within & Without

A Time for Compassion

Lost & Found

Let Your Heart Pray

All published by Don Bosco Publications
Thornleigh House
Sharples Park
BOLTON BL1 6PQ
Email: **joyce@salesians.org.uk**
www.don-bosco-publications.co.uk

OTHER DON BOSCO PUBLICATIONS

A SWATCH JOURNEY THROUGH LENT	T Passerello & D O'Malley
SWATCH & PRAY A new concept prayer book for young people	D O'Malley
SCHOOL ETHOS & CHAPLAINCY	D O'Malley
THE CHRISTIAN TEACHER	D O'Malley
CHRISTIAN LEADERSHIP	D O'Malley
ORDINARY WAYS	D O'Malley
PRAYERS TO CLOSE THE DAY	D O'Malley
PRAYERS TO START THE DAY	D O'Malley
TRUST THE ROAD 3rd edition with coloured illustrations	D O'Malley
VIA LUCIS The Stations of the Resurrection	D O'Malley
STARTING AGAIN FROM DON BOSCO	I Murdoch
SERVING THE YOUNG Our Catholic Schools Today	J Gallagher
DVD ROSIE GOES TO CHURCH A child's guide to the church	K Pearce
BOOK ROSIE GOES TO CHURCH A child's guide to the church	K Pearce
CHLOE AND JACK VISIT THE VATICAN	K Pearce
GOOD NEWS IN THE FAMILY The life of Jesus in story form	K Pearce
OUR COLOURFUL CHURCH YEAR	K Pearce
101 SAINTS AND SPECIAL PEOPLE Lives of Saints for children	K Pearce
SEAN DEVEREUX—A life given for Africa 1964-1993	M Delmer
LENTEN SUNDAYS Reflections on the Gospel Readings.	M Winstanley
DON BOSCO'S GOSPEL WAY	M Winstanley
SYMBOLS and SPIRITUALITY reflecting on John's Gospel	M Winstanley
GOD OF MANY FACES Reflective verses	M Renshaw
MOVING ON Book of reflective poetry	Margaret J Cooke
MAMMA MARGARET The Life of Don Bosco's Mother	T Bosco
TEACHER, TEACH US TO PRAY for use in primary schools	W Acred
THE WITNESSES	W Acred
DON'T ORGANISE MY TEARS Reflections on bereavement	A Bailey
BOSCO Z-BOOK	A Bailey